MASTERING

PRACTICAL WRITING

MACMILLAN MASTER SERIES

Banking
Basic Management
Biology
British Politics
Business Communication
Business Microcomputing
Chemistry
COBOL Programming
Commerce
Computer Programming
Computers
Data Processing
Economics
Electonics
English Grammar
English Language
English Literature
Financial Accounting
French
French 2
German
Hairdressing

Italian
Keyboarding
Marketing
Mathematics
Modern British History
Modern World History
Nutrition
Office Practice
Pascal Programming
Physics
Practical Writing
Principles of Accounts
Social Welfare
Sociology
Spanish
Spanish 2
Statistics
Statistics withYour Microcomputer
Study Skills
Typewriting Skills
Word Processing

MASTERING
PRACTICAL
WRITING

S. H. BURTON

MACMILLAN
EDUCATION

First published 1987

Published by
MACMILLAN EDUCATION LTD
Houndmills, Basingstoke, Hampshire RG21 2XS
and London
Companies and representatives
throughout the world

Typeset by Tecset Ltd,
Wallington, Surrey

Printed in Hong Kong

British Library Cataloguing in Publication Data
Burton, S.H.
Mastering practical writing. —
(Macmillan master series)
1. English language — Composition and exercises
I. Title
808'.042'076   PE1413
ISBN 0-333-39858-0
ISBN 0-333-39859-9 Pbk
ISBN 0-333-39860-2 Pbk export

CONTENTS

We may not want to write, but we know we must.

PREFACE

Most of us do as little writing as possible, but there are many jobs we can't escape. Our work and the necessary business transactions of our private life push us into doing them. We may not want to write, but we know we must. If we don't, some practical matter that concerns us won't be attended to. So, however reluctantly, we tackle these pieces of writing because we need to get something done.

Practical writing is regarded as a chore (and it frequently *is*), but it must be done well. Though it is often about humdrum, routine subjects, they always matter. Otherwise, we wouldn't put ourselves to the trouble of writing about them!

Our readers' response to the way we write materially affects our everyday lives. Practical concerns are helped on or held back by the efficiency or inefficiency of our writing.

If you make full use of the help this book offers, it will show you how to improve your practical writing. To make sure that you do use it to best advantage, notice these four special features before you begin:

1 It is a *course* in practical writing, and you must work your way through it. Don't sit back, passively reading. Get to grips with all the examples, and work out all the exercises. They are designed to teach you how to write, but you won't learn if you don't do them.
2 The notes and answers in Chapter 7 will help you to profit from – even, perhaps, enjoy – the exercises. Work out your own answers before you look at mine. One of the best ways of learning to write is to compare your efforts with someone else's. It is very important to explore various ways of tackling problems, finding out why one way works better than another. (My way won't always be better than yours.)
3 As a glance down the list of contents shows, this book is about the bedrock problems that writing involves. It helps you to understand exactly what you are trying to do when you write. It examines the demands that writing makes. It explores attitudes, approaches and responses.

Correct grammar, punctuation, spelling and layout are important. You can't write well without those skills; but you can still write very badly with them. It's putting the cart before the horse to concentrate on 'the mechanics' before you've thought hard about writing in the ways suggested here.

Help with grammar, punctuation and the other similar matters that I have not attempted to cover here is readily available. *Mastering English*

Grammar and *Mastering English Language* (both published by Macmillan) are reliable guides to these important skills. The help that this book gives you is of a different kind. It is about identifying targets and learning how to hit them. If you take aim at the wrong target, even perfect literacy cannot guide your writing to its proper mark.

4 In each chapter, writing is considered 'in the round'. The main emphasis may be on one particular aspect of the writing process – writer/reader relationship, orderly arrangement, appropriate language, and so on – but no attempt is made to isolate the immediate topic by boxing it up inside the boundaries of that one chapter. There is continuous and planned cross-fertilisation between chapter and chapter, reflecting the realities of writing. That is why, for example, the basic issues raised in Chapter 1 are never allowed to drop out of sight, and why the contents of Sections 2.2 and 4.1 are interwoven.

To write well, you have to be able to respond simultaneously to the demands made by a complex set of circumstances. And that is why writing cannot be 'explained' in a series of self-contained 'lessons'.

S.H.B.

FROM *A* TO *B*

1.1 GETTING THINGS DONE

Practical writing is often referred to as *transactional* writing. That is a good description, because the subject is always some 'business' that Person *A* (the writer) has in hand with Person *B* (the reader). The purpose of such writing is to carry that practical matter - that 'transaction' - forward in some way. It is the essentially *functional* nature of practical writing that makes it different from personal and creative writing.

- Practical writing is the kind of writing that tries to get things done.

1.2 GETTING ON WELL TOGETHER

Things are likely to get done when the people involved in them get on well together - or, as we often say, when they understand each other. A good working relationship depends very largely on good communication. If Person *B* cannot understand something that Person *A* says or writes, or is 'put off' by the way it is said or written, the practical matter that they have in hand is obstructed. The words that were intended to be a bridge between them have acted as a barrier instead.

Think of 'communication' as *message-sending* - for that is what we are trying to do when we attempt to communicate. Then the importance of good communication can be explained in very simple terms:

- The better we are are at sending messages to other people, the easier it is to get on well with them and to get things done.

1.3 GETTING THE MESSAGE THROUGH

(a) Mind reading

When we are writing, we are up against one particular difficulty that does not arise when we are speaking. Speaking to somebody face-to-face or on the telephone, we can tell while we are speaking how the other person is reacting to our words. We know whether our message is getting through. But when we are writing to someone, we cannot get that kind of help. We are not in immediate, direct contact, so we have to guess how the other person will react to our words and whether our message will get through. We have to try to read our reader's mind!

(b) No second chance

Face-to-face, our listener provides us with vital signals which tell us a lot about his/her reactions to what we are saying. Smiles, frowns, nods, gestures and movements indicate agreement or disagreement, enthusiasm or hostility, interest or boredom – and so on.

We don't get visual signals on the phone, of course, but both then and face-to-face our listener comes back at us with remarks such as 'Good', 'Go on', 'Perhaps', 'Really?'. And wordless but 'translatable' noises such as *Mm, Uh?, Hmph!* provide other kinds of indications of how things are going. Often, too, our listener intervenes with explicit expressions of his/her immediate reactions: 'I don't understand.' – 'Yes, that's clear.' – 'Are you sure?'.

If our listener's signals tell us that our message is not getting through, we can try there and then to improve it. We can re-word parts that our listener has not understood. We can rearrange the order of items. We can deal with objections. We can adopt a different tone of voice. Speaking a message gives us immediate opportunities of recovering from a bad start.

But when we are writing, the situation gives us no such opportunities. No signals are coming back to indicate our reader's reactions. By the time our message is being read, it has passed out of our control. Unless we have anticipated our reader's reactions accurately, we have failed. The message has not got through in the way we intended, and there is nothing we can do about it.

- While we are speaking, we *know* how the other person *is reacting*. While we are writing, we have to try to *anticipate* how the other person *will react*.

Exercise 1

(a) Recall a conversation (either face-to-face or on the telephone) in the course of which you realised that you were not getting through to the other person in the way you intended. Then examine that experience in detail by answering these questions.

(i) How did the other person make you realise that you were not getting through? Try to remember exactly what signals (verbal/non-verbal/visual) he/she sent you.

How did the other person make you realise that you were not getting through?

(ii) Why were you failing? Think it out. Perhaps the cause was one or more of these:
    (a) Your listener reacted to your choice of words or your tone of voice in a way that you did not expect or want.
    (b) Your listener did not understand a particular word (or particular words) that you were using.
    (c) Your listener needed information that you had not supplied.
    (d) Your listener could not understand or did not like your way of expressing yourself.
    Perhaps it was some other cause? Try to analyse your failure and to describe it in detail.

(iii) When your listener signalled that you were not getting through, were you then able to put things right? If so, how did your second attempt differ from your first? If you still could not get through, why was that?

(b) When the response to a message we have written shows us that we failed to get through, the fault may not have been ours. Often, however, we realise that we *could* have written a successful message had we tried harder to anticipate our reader's reactions to what we wrote. Try to recall in detail an example of your own failure to write a successful message. These headings will help you to think about it clearly.

    (i) Identity of person to whom your message was written.
    (ii) Subject matter of message.

(iii) Form of message (note - postcard - letter - memorandum - report - other).

(iv) Response you hoped for when writing the message.

(v) Cause/causes of your failure to obtain the desired response.

(vi) Changes you would make if you were writing the message again.

1.4 WRITER AND READER

(a) Writing for readers we know

Getting a written message through is very much a matter of striking the right note. That is why it is so important to try to anticipate the reader's reactions.

When we are writing to a member of our family or to a friend, we are well placed to read our reader's mind. We know a lot about him/her as a person, so we have a pretty good idea of how he/she will react, and we can choose our words in the light of that foreknowledge.

We may be writing to such a reader about some practical matter - say, a meeting we want to arrange, or a favour we want to ask - but the 'transaction' is taking place between a writer and a reader who have a personal relationship. While we are writing, we have a fund of previously acquired knowledge and understanding on which we can rely. Unless we are careless, clumsy or insensitive, it should not be too difficult to choose words that will strike the right note.

(b) Writing for readers we do not know

Many of the practical matters that we have to deal with in writing are conducted with readers we do not know. Often, we do not even know their names. We know only the positions they hold and the jobs they do. Indeed, our sole reason for communicating with them is the fact that, because of the positions they hold and the jobs they do, we need to involve them in whatever particular transaction it is that we are writing about.

It is just as important to anticipate the reactions of a reader we do not know as to anticipate the reactions of a reader we do know. Obviously, if our message fails to get through because the reader does not understand its contents or is put off by the way it is written, the practical things we are writing about will not get done.

If we anticipate the reader's reactions, we can avoid potential blunders and correct mistakes before they can do any harm. We can reject material that the reader is likely to misunderstand or consider irrelevant. We can amend phrasing that would be tactless or objectionable.

Reading the mind of a reader we do not know - for that is what we have to do - may seem a very tall order, but it is by no means as difficult as it sounds. We have little knowledge of our reader to guide our choice of words but, for the purpose of practical writing, *we do not need it*. We are not in a personal relationship with our reader, so our choice of words is guided by quite different considerations.

We are writing about a particular and clearly defined subject. It is some practical matter - some piece of business, some transaction - that we are trying to get done. We are writing to a particular person, but only because his/her official position or job involves him/her in that matter.

- The circumstances of practical writing place the writer and the reader in an *impersonal* relationship.

In a very real way, an impersonal writer/reader relationship makes it easy for us to anticipate our reader's reactions. There are two reasons for this. First, we do not have to rack our brains to think of things to write about. The contents of a practical message are very largely determined for us by the transaction in hand. Second, we have a much narrower choice of suitable ways of expressing those contents than in personal or creative writing. Practical (impersonal) writing has its own conventions, and our reader expects us to observe them.

So, knowing what our reader's expectations are, we have clear standards by which we can anticipate the likely effect of our words.

That is why it is not so very difficult to read an unknown reader's mind.

- Unlike personal and creative writing, practical (impersonal) writing is regulated by well known and generally accepted conventions which provide the writer with guidelines.

Exercise 2
Here are six examples (some practical, some personal) of various kinds of everyday writing jobs.

TO	PURPOSE
(a) your grandmother, or some other elderly relative	to send birthday greetings
(b) one of your lecturers	to get his/her advice on a problem arising from your choice of subjects
(c) a travel agent	to ask for further details of a holiday
(d) a prospective employer	to apply for a job

(e) a friend of your own age who lives at a distance	to arrange a meeting
(f) your boss at work	to summarise newspaper report of a council meeting at which planning regulations that may affect your firm were discussed

Think about each of those tasks along the lines indicated below. Choose the answers (suggested inside the brackets) that correspond to your ideas. But feel free to add to or to alter the suggested answers if you can describe the writing jobs more accurately by doing so.

(i)   Your *relationship with your reader* is (personal – impersonal).

(ii) Your *motive for writing* is that (you want to – you have to – you feel you ought to – you need to).

(iii) Your *attitude to your reader* is (loving – friendly – distant – neutral – hostile).

(iv) You (do – do not) *intend to make your reader aware of your attitude to him/her.*

(v)   It is (difficult – not very difficult – easy) *to find things to write about.*

(vi) It is (difficult – not very difficult – easy) *to find a suitable way of writing.*

(vii) The *most difficult* of those tasks is – , because – .

(viii) The *easiest* of those tasks is – , because – .

1.5 READER AND WRITER

Every message you write – note, report, letter, postcard, memorandum – is an attempt to communicate with another person. Even when the contents of the message and your purpose in writing it are strictly practical, and even when you have little or no personal knowledge of your reader, you are *getting in touch with somebody.* That 'somebody' – that other *person* – is going to react to what you have written and to the way you have written it. In so doing, he/she will form an impression of the sort of person you are.

The quality of your writing always tells your reader something about you. Sometimes, it tells quite a lot. For example, your knowledge of a particular subject, your ability to think clearly about it, and the soundness of your opinions on it may be revealed.

What all your practical writing is bound to tell your reader is whether you are efficient and tactful or muddle-headed and inconsiderate in your dealings with other people.

So, although practical writing is functional and impersonal, your reader will always form a view of what sort of a person you are.

- That view may well determine your reader's willingness and/or ability to respond to your message in the way you hoped when you wrote it.

Your reader will always form a view of what sort of person you are.

1.6 **THINKING IT OUT**

Never start on a piece of practical writing until you have thought out the answers to these questions:

1 Who is my reader? What official position does he/she hold? What job does he/she do? How is he/she involved in the matter I am going to write about?
2 Why am I going to write this message for this person to read? What am I trying to achieve by writing it?
3 Exactly what do I need to include in this particular message to this particular reader to achieve this particular result?

You cannot decide on a suitable way of writing – an appropriate style – until you have found the answers to those questions. (See Section 1.7 and Chapters 3 and 4.)

1.7 GOOD WRITING: A SUMMARY

Careful consideration of the reader's needs and expectations is the basis of good practical writing. Its essential qualities are:

1 clear organisation and clear expression;
2 relevant contents;
3 an appropriate style.

The first two of those qualities meet the reader's needs. The third satisfies the reader's expectations.

(a) Clarity

Clear arrangement and expression are of the first importance. A message that is not understood – or is not understood in the way the writer meant it to be – cannot bring about the desired response.

Good writing, however, is not merely comprehensible: it is *readily* comprehensible. It is as easy to read and to understand as circumstances permit.

However complicated your subject matter may be, you must help your reader by avoiding all unnecessary difficulties. He/she will not feel co-operative if your message is harder to understand than it need have been.

- It is always in the writer's interest to make the reader's task as easy as possible.

(b) Relevance

Every item of the contents must be relevant to the matter in hand. If you don't keep to the point you are wasting your reader's time (and your own). You are also making your message hard to read and to understand. Irrelevant material causes muddle and misunderstanding.

(c) Appropriate (suitable) style

All practical writing is functional and the writer/reader relationship is impersonal, but different situations call for different ways of writing (different styles). What is suitable in one set of circumstances is unsuitable in another.

For example, suppose you want to follow up this advertisement in your local paper:

D.I.Y SHOWER KITS

No need to pay to have it done.
Complete range of kits and parts in stock.
Free instruction manual.
s.a.e. for details.
Unit 6, Dale Street, Runthorpe, RU2 6DS.

A note such as this would be suitable:

D.I.Y SHOWER KITS

Please send details, as advertised in *Runthorpe Gazette* (25/11/-)
J. Brown, 52 Acre Terrace, Runthorpe, RU4 8AT

But that streamlined form of message and very brief way of writing would be unsuitable in a different situation - for example, when writing to ask the admissions tutor of a college to send you details of a course for which you hope to enrol. Though you have 'business' to transact, and though your relationship with your reader is impersonal, that situation requires you to use the formal courtesies appropriate to a well-expressed letter of request.

(d) Summing up
Good writing does not come by chance. You must go about it thoughfully and methodically, taking all these considerations into account:

1 You are writing:
  - to a particular *reader*, R;
  - on a particular *occasion*, O;
  - about a particular *subject*, S;
  - for a particular *purpose*, P.
2 Before you begin to write a message, you have to decide on:
  - its *contents*;
  - its *form*;
  - its *style*.
3 Only by thinking carefully about your reader, the occasion, your subject, and your purpose *(ROSP)*, can you ensure that:
  - the contents of your message are *relevant*;
  - the form of your message is *suitable*;
  - the style of your message is *appropriate*.

Exercise 3
(a) The next two examples, drawn from my own experience of practical writing, illustrate the points made in Section 1.7(d). Notice in each how the writer's awareness of the particular circumstances (writer/reader relationship, occasion, subject, and purpose) influences the selection of relevant subject matter and the choice of an appropriate style.

(i) The inspector who deals with my income tax lives just down the road from me. I do not know him well, but we pass the time of day when I walk past his garden, in which he spends a lot of his spare time. I, too, am a keen gardener. Two or three times a year I have to write practical - very practical! - messages to him at his office, either to raise taxation matters with him or to reply to matters that he has raised with me. When I am writing those letters, I do not consider it relevant to refer to our acquaintanceship or to our shared interest in gardening. (That decision is in line with the fact that neither of us refers to our official correspondence when we are chatting.) When I write to him, I try to be crisp and business-like - though, of course, polite. Writing in a formal style, I keep strictly to the matters in hand. I always begin: 'Dear Sir', and I always end: 'Yours faithfully'.

(ii) Recently, I wrote a letter to the director of our local leisure centre (whom I do not know at all), suggesting that she tried to book a popular jazz group for the coming season of concerts. This was a practical message, for I was writing it to get something done. My relationship with my reader was impersonal, for I was writing to her in her official capacity. Indeed, I wouldn't have been writing to her at all but for the job she does. I was writing to her in my official capacity - as a ratepayer who helps to support the leisure centre. Nevertheless, I wrote this letter in a less formal style than the letters I write to the inspector of taxes. For example, I began: 'Dear Ms —' and I ended: 'Yours sincerely'. And I considered it relevant to refer to her own admiration for that particular jazz group, which I knew from an article of hers I happened to have read in a music magazine.

(b) Suppose you have to write a request to a person in some official position. You may perhaps be asking permission to take a particular course of action - say, wanting to drop one college subject and take up another in its place. The details are up to you, but they should be drawn from your own experience. Consider how the particular circumstances of that situation would influence your decisions about what to write and how to write it.

Work it out along these lines:

CIRCUMSTANCES TO BE CONSIDERED

1 Your relationship with your reader.
2 The nature of the occasion on which you are writing.
3 The subject about which you are writing.
4 Your purpose in writing and, therefore, the response that you want your reader to make.

DECISIONS TO BE TAKEN

1 Contents of message - what is relevant?

2 Suitable form for message - note, letter, postcard, memorandum, and so on.
3 Appropriate style of writing - see Examples a(i) and a(ii) in this exercise

CHAPTER 2

IF I WERE YOU

2.1 SWITCHING ROUND

Many difficulties, delays and misunderstandings can be avoided by putting yourself in your reader's place. So, if you want to save yourself (and your reader) time and trouble, switch round and read your message through your reader's eyes.

- Never send a written message without looking at it critically, asking yourself: 'How would I react to this, if I were you?'

Exercise 1

In the incident described below a message went wrong because its writer failed to see it through its reader's eyes. Taking all the circumstances into account, how would you have avoided the mistake I made?

I was expecting a visitor to arrive at four o'clock one afternoon. She does a lot of typing for me, so we know each other quite well within our working relationship. However, as I always take my manuscripts to her office and collect the typescripts, she had never been to my house before. On this particular occasion, I had asked her to call to pick up a chapter that required special treatment.

At quarter to four, I had a phone call that made it necessary for me to go out for a short time. I hastily arranged with a neighbour to let my visitor into my house. Then I scribbled a note, which I left on the hall table:

Sorry, I've had to go out. Back by 4.30. Tea in tin on shelf in kitchen. Biscuits in cupboard. Please help yourself.

I did not get back until quarter to five. My visitor had gone, but she had left a note beside mine:

Which tin? Which shelf? Which cupboard?

4.30 – couldn't wait any longer. Have taken MS. Will ring you this evening, about 6. Thanks for the invitation. But which tin? Which shelf? Which cupboard? Still, it was a kind thought!

I had three purposes when I wrote my message: to explain and apologise for my absence; to tell my visitor when I would be back; to enable her to help herself to some refreshment while she waited. I succeeded in the first two, but I failed in the third because I did not supply all the information she needed. There are several shelves in my kitchen, with several tins on each, and there are several cupboards. I knew which tin contained tea and which cupboard the biscuits were in, but she did not. To find out, she would have to rummage through my kitchen. We did not know each other well enough for her to feel comfortable about doing that.

Had I read my note (and looked at my kitchen!) with my reader's eyes, I'd have written better. As it was, because I didn't switch round, that part of my message failed to get through.

Though the inefficiency of the writing had no serious consequences on that particular occasion, considerable – and sometimes long-lasting – damage can be caused by a writer's failure to look at a message from its reader's point of view.

Switching round helps the writer to avoid these three common mistakes:

- leaving out essential material;
- getting off the point;
- using an unsuitable style.

2.2 CONTENTS, ORDER, STYLE

Correctly-constructed sentences, accurate punctuation and spelling are essential. You cannot write well unless you are competent in those skills; but technical competence alone does not make good writing. Faultless manipulation of 'the mechanics' is of little help when you have not thought out exactly *what* you are trying to do – and *why* you are doing it – and *how* best to do it.

As you will see, there is little, if anything, wrong with the sentences, vocabulary, punctuation and spelling of the pieces of writing in the exercises that now follow. Even so, they are not well written. The particular demands made by the nature of the job to be done were not thought out. Correct but undirected writing left the reader's justifiable expectations unsatisfied.

Note Suggested answers to Exercises 2, 3 and 4 are provided in Chapter 7. Do *not* look at them until you have worked through the exercises on your own. Try to find out for yourself where and how these writers went wrong.

The *Guidelines* in the exercises show you how to work out your answers. Having done that, compare them with mine.

Exercise 2
Read the following extracts. What mistakes did these two writers make? Consider each passage with the help of the *Guidelines*, and then compare your answers with the comments provided in Chapter 7.

(a) *Extract from the annual 'Newsletter' sent out to all members of a social club. This item was headed: 'Secretary's Notes – Subscriptions'.*

Members are asked to notice the following changes as from 1 November last year. 1. The club's financial year will run from 1 May to 30 April every year, as resolved at the AGM on 31 October last. 2. In future, the date of the AGM will be moved nearer to the beginning of the club's financial year to permit the treasurer to present final figures for the end of the financial year and, also in accordance with an AGM resolution (31 October, last) this will, in practice, mean the first Saturday of every year following the first of May every year. 3. Subscriptions will, therefore, fall due not on 1 January of each year, as in past years, but on 1 May of future years, except this year, when subscriptions paid as in the past on 1 January will be deemed to have been paid for the year as if it began on 1 May. Any member having problems should get in touch with either the treasurer or the secretary, by telephone. It was also resolved on 31 October that there is to be no change in the rate of subscription for this coming year, commencing on 1 May.

Guidelines
  (i) What evidence can you find in the secretary's *Notes* to show that he did or that he did not put himself in his reader's place while he was writing them?
 (ii) Reading the *Notes* as a member of the club, which two items of information would be of most importance to you?
(iii) Do those two items stand out clearly in the *Notes*?
 (iv) Did the secretary arrange the various items in a sensible order? If you think not, suggest a better order.
  (v) If you think that paragraphing would help the reader, suggest where new paragraphs should begin.

(b) *Extract from a letter sent by one friend to another*

... Yes, it's Jean! Out of the blue, I know, but I've just learnt that I've got a day off next week, so I thought I'd try to see you and Jan again. I could catch the 06.30 from Carlisle and, if you could meet me at Euston, we could go to Jan's together and be there by 11.30. It would be nice if we all had lunch together before going to the theatre, but of course I don't know how Jan will be placed. It's my treat, but I want you to get the tickets. It's easier for you, living in London, but I'll pay. I can't stay overnight, but I needn't leave until the eight o'clock train. Plenty of time to do everything. I'll leave you to get in touch with Jan about all this, and let me know. I'll only confuse things if I write to her as well. It will be so nice to see you both again. I've got lots of news, but it must wait. I'm off on a course tomorrow, and I'll be away until the day before my trip to London (back early evening). I think I explained on my Christmas card that I've got this job with . . .

Guidelines

(i) Judging by the style, what sort of a relationship does the writer feel she has with her reader?

(ii) The writer is trying to get several things done. Does she make them clear?

(iii) Consider the way in which she organises the transactional part of her letter. And does she tell her reader all she needs to know?

(iv) Put yourself in the recipient's place and try to imagine what her reactions were when she read this letter.

Exercise 3

The passage of writing on which this exercise is based is an extract from a candidate's answer to the examination question printed below. Study the answer with the help of the *Guidelines*, and comment on the quality of the candidate's writing. Then compare your views with the comments provided in Chapter 7.

Examination Question

Give an account of any one of Britain's various attempts to renegotiate the terms of its EEC membership.

Extract from candidate's answer

It was in the spring of 1974 that the British government made its most serious attempt to renegotiate terms that were generally resented by the British people. At least, it said that it was attempting a thorough revision of the terms, but I take that with a pinch of salt, myself. There were four particular issues in question, and enough was done to make it appear that there had been real changes. Certainly, the government pushed hard to get a 'Yes' vote in the referendum it held in 1975. It got just over 67 per cent of the voters - of those who bothered to vote, that is - to agree. The four areas of renegotiation at that time were the Common Agricultural Policy, the level of Britain's contributions to the Community Budget, though neither of these got really settled and have gone on being argued about, and trade with and aid to the countries of the British Commonwealth and developing countries, and the vexed question of whether EEC regulations overrode Britain's right to pursue independent regional and industrial policies were also included. I'm not at all sure it wouldn't have been better not to threaten to leave the EEC if satisfaction could not be obtained, for the drama of that threat stopped work on revisions of CAP as a whole that were already going on, and by concentrating on the immediate issue of Britain's CAP difficulties a chance was lost to effect a thorough reform of the whole thing. In fact, as it turned out, you could sum up the 1974–75 renegotiations as a lot of fuss about nothing in particular - only, I suppose, it looked different at the time.

Guidelines
   (i)   Judging by this extract, the candidate knows quite a lot about the subject, but do you think that he/she makes good use of that knowledge? What have you to say about the order in which the various items are presented?
   (ii) Bearing in mind the writer/reader relationship, what have you to say about the style of the writing?
  (iii) Think about these two questions: (a) What qualities do you think an examiner expects to find in a candidate's writing? (b) How far do you think this candidate's writing satisfies those expectations?

Exercise 4
Read the following examples. What mistakes did each of the writers make? Answer as fully as you can before looking at the comments in Chapter 7.

(a) *Extract from a student's letter to a lecturer*

I thought you'd better know from me before you see next term's list that I'm dropping maths. It's not that I think the subject's useless or that I think you can't teach it. It's not the subject or you - it's me! I'm not exactly Einstein and I'll never be able to cope with an advanced course in maths. I've got my 'O' level pass, and that's my lot. It's all I'll ever need - or be up to. So, thanks for trying. You'll probably be relieved to see the back of me.

(b) *Extract from an essay written during a course in environmental studies*

This awareness of impending crisis has quickened interest in four major areas of environmental concern: population, pollution, food, and energy; for it is widely realised that the quality of life depends on the interaction of all four, and on our ability to exert rational and co-ordinated control over them. The hottest topic of the lot is the sun – a joke that happens to be serious, as I shall now show.

(c) *A questionnaire circulated to all ratepayers by the chief executive officer of a borough council drew this response to one of the questions*

My answer to this is an emphatic 'NO'. I'm against spending money on the borough theatre. Give reasons, you say. I'll give you mine in a nutshell. The borough council and its officers are completely out of touch with ordinary people. I'm totally cheesed off with the so-called 'entertainments' I've been forced to subsidise. 'He who pays the piper calls the tune', my old father used to say. I shudder to think what he'd say about the concerts you've been putting on. Diabolical!

(d) *Extract from a 'thank you' letter written to a grandparent*

Thank you for the card and for the kind gift that accompanied it. They arrived on my birthday, and as that was only yesterday, you can see that I have wasted no time in informing you.

Guidelines
  (i) The headings indicate the circumstances in which each of those passages was written.
  (ii) Taking the circumstances into account (especially the writer/reader relationship), comment on the style of each passage.

2.3 CONSIDERATION, CLARITY, PERSUASIVENESS

Your particular and immediate reasons for undertaking a practical writing task vary from one occasion to another, just as the particular forms of the messages you have to write vary – letters, notes, memoranda, reports, and so on.

But every piece of writing you have to do is well done or badly done in so far as it achieves or fails to achieve the two basic aims of all writing:

- To express your meaning clearly.
- To persuade your reader to respond in the way you want.

The examples you studied in the exercises in Section 2.2 were written on different occasions and for different reasons. Each was literate, but — to a greater or lesser degree — each failed to reach a satisfactory standard of clarity and/or persuasiveness. In each case, the message did not get through because the writer was insensitive to the reader's needs and expectations.

If you put yourself in your reader's place, you will be much more likely to succeed in:

- organising your subject matter clearly;
- finding a suitable style.

Then, having done your best to make your meaning plain and to write in a way that does not jar or distract, you have done everything possible to deserve your reader's attention and co-operation.

CHAPTER 3

WHEN? WHAT? WHY?

Section 1.7(d) listed the four circumstances you have to take into account whenever you have a practical writing job to do: your relationship with your reader; the particular occasion on which you are writing; the subject about which you are writing; the purpose for which you are writing (*ROSP*).

The writer/reader relationship and its implications were explored in Chapters 1 and 2, so we can now turn to the others.

Bear in mind, however, that although it is helpful to discuss each of these circumstances separately, *in practice* they all work together. It is their *combined* influence that determines a successful choice of contents, form and style. Whenever and whatever you are writing, all four of these circumstances come into play. Each affects the others.

That is why the explanations and exercises in Chapters 1 and 2 had to include considerations of occasion, subject matter and purpose, though their starting-point was the writer/reader relationship. In Exercise 3 of Chapter 1, for example, though the writer/reader relationships were similar, differences of occasion, subject matter and purpose made one style of writing appropriate to one letter and a different style appropriate to the other.

3.1 FORMAL AND INFORMAL OCCASIONS

Awareness of the nature of the occasion influences (or should influence) the writer's selection of contents and choice of style. Good sentences, vocabulary, punctuation and spelling are of no avail when the contents and style are inappropriate to the occasion.

For example, the examination candidate whose answer you studied in Chapter 2 (Exercise 3) wrote badly because he got the writer/reader relationship wrong; and he got that wrong because he misjudged the nature of the occasion on which he was writing. Personal opinions expressed

Awareness of the nature of the occasion . . .

informally would have been suitable had the writing occasion been informal (a letter to a friend, for instance). As it was - the writing occasion being strictly formal - an objective presentation of facts in a formal style was called for.

Exercise 1

Heating problems in the office in which Jane Smith works have been causing inconvenience for some time. Jane's immediate superior, who works in a different room, has given her the following instructions:

1 Let me have have any suggestions you can make to improve things while the repairs are going on. On one side of an A5 memo sheet, and by five this evening, please.
2 Go through the Everwarm Engineering file and prepare a summary of our dealings with them over the past two months. Let me have it by the end of the week so that I'm briefed on the matter when I see the office manager next Tuesday.

Consider carefully the two writing jobs that Jane Smith has to do. Note their similarities and differences by analysing each under the headings: *reader*; *occasion*; *subject matter*; *purpose*. Note especially how the two jobs differ in the degree of formality that they impose on the writer. That difference between them will influence Jane's decisions about the contents, form and style of each piece of writing.

Whenever you have a practical writing job to do, it is important to make an accurate assessment of the formality of the occasion. That assessment plays a major part in ensuring that you write relevantly and in an appropriate style.

- You cannot strike the right note if you misjudge the degree of formality appropriate to the occasion.

3.2 **THE PROBLEM OF RELEVANCE**

It is easy (and true) to state that an essential quality of good practical writing is the relevance of its contents, but it is not always easy in practice to decide what is relevant and what is not. We all experience difficulty at times in knowing what to include and what to exclude.

Take the first of Jane Smith's two tasks (Section 3.1) as an example. When making her suggestions, she probably had to question whether some of her ideas were relevant to the job she had been given. Suppose she thought that some of her colleagues ought to wear warmer clothes while the heating problems lasted. Would that be a relevant item to include in the brief note for which her boss had asked? Or suppose she thought that the firm ought to pay extra to employees working in that office under those conditions. Would that be relevant?

Of course, you cannot answer those questions without studying her boss's instructions very carefully and trying to decide exactly what she meant by asking for 'suggestions . . . to improve things'. Did she mean 'to make the office more comfortable'? Did she mean 'to keep the office work going smoothly'? Did she mean 'to compensate the employees for their trials'?

Knowing her boss, Jane may have been in no doubt what she meant. If she was not clear she would be sensible to ask for an explanation before attempting the task.

Now consider the second of those writing jobs. Jane was told to provide her boss with 'a summary of our dealings with them [Everwarm Engineering] over the past two months'. When she was reading through the file she would find notes of phone calls and copies of memoranda and letters, all coming under the general heading of 'dealings with' Everwarm Engineering, but concerned with various matters. She would then have a problem. Should she summarise *all* her firm's dealings with Everwarm during the period specified by her boss? Or should she summarise solely those matters arising out of the office heating problems?

Since her boss was readily accessible, she would probably ask her whether she required a general summary of the firm's dealings with Everwarm or a selective summary limited to that one particular aspect of those dealings.

If she had not been able to ask for clarification, she would have had to reason it out for herself. Her thinking would proceed along these lines:

1 I've been told to summarise our dealings with Everwarm Engineering over the past two months.
2 But I was given that job because we've been experiencing heating problems in this office during that period.
3 It is those problems that my boss will be discussing with the office manager next Tuesday.
4 Therefore, *in these circumstances*, only matters connected with the heating problems are relevant.
5 I shall write a *selective* summary of the contents of the file, covering everything that is connected with our heating problems and excluding all other matters.

Practical writing is concerned with 'business' – with transactions – with matters about which the writer is trying to get something done. That is why it is so important to ensure that everything you include is relevant. Irrelevant material fogs the issue. It confuses and/or irritates your reader, making him/her much less likely to be able or willing to respond to your writing in the way you want.

Irrelevant material fogs the issue.

As the examples just studied demonstrate – and as your own experience will show – you often have to think hard when you are trying to decide what is relevant – and what is not.

When you are writing, weigh each item against this definition before you decide to include it:

- *relevant* – bearing upon the matter in hand.

3.3 **THE MATTER IN HAND**

Provided you understand exactly what is meant by *the matter in hand*, that definition of 'relevant' provides the guidance you need when you are trying to decide what to put in and what to leave out.

Every piece of writing you have to do falls within some general 'subject area' or other. In other words, it is 'about something'! But *exactly what* is it about? It is much too vague to say, 'I'm writing to the travel agents about my holiday', when your real 'target' is to find out whether you can get better terms if you go in October instead of in July.

Every 'subject' has to be narrowed down from general description to a precise identification of 'the matter in hand'. Only then can you discover a *sense of direction* to steer you through the job you have to do. An over-simplified view of your 'subject' is bound to result in waffly writing.

Jane Smith (see Sections 3.1 and 3.2) was told that her 'subject' was her firm's dealings with a heating company, but she could not write efficiently until she had narrowed it down and pinpointed the matter in hand.

Similarly, all my letters to the inspector of taxes (see Section 1.7) have one general subject in common: my income tax affairs. But whenever I write to him, I have to be quite clear which particular aspect of that subject is uppermost. One letter may be about my claim for a tax rebate for a year in which I was over-assessed. Another may be about an entry in my accounts for heavier-than-usual expenditure on business stationery. Both those letters have the same general subject: my income tax. But each is specifically concerned with a distinctly different aspect of that general subject; and in each case, I am trying to get different things done. Material that would be relevant in one would be irrelevant in the other.

In every practical writing job, the matter you have in hand is that particular aspect of a subject which you are bringing to the attention of a particular reader, on a particular occasion, for a particular purpose.

So, whenever you are having difficulty in deciding what to include, put the doubtful material to the test, like this:

- If I bring this item (fact, suggestion, idea, opinion, argument – whatever it is)

- to the attention of this reader
- on this occasion
- will it/will it not help me to achieve the purpose for which I am writing?

3.4 **DIRECTED WRITING**

Think out the exact purpose for which you are writing before you begin. If you are woolly-minded about your objective you cannot direct your writing accurately, and you will miss your target oftener than you will hit it.

Most practical writing has one (or more than one) of the following as its objective:

- to supply information;
- to give instructions or to make requests;
- to persuade its reader to act in some way;
- to influence its reader's attitude to/judgement of/opinions about the the matter in hand.

In practice, those objectives often overlap, but it is essential to make up your mind which of them – separately or in combination – is uppermost in any particular job. If you think out exactly what you are trying to do, you will then see how to arrange the contents in a clear and sensible way. (See Chapter 4.)

Study the following exercises. They are based on typical examples of practical writing, and they take up and illustrate points made earlier in this and preceding chapters. In each exercise, a practical writing job is carefully thought out. Contents, form and style are considered in relation to the particular circumstances (reader, occasion, subject matter and purpose) of the different situations in which the writers are placed.

Exercise 2
Jack Jones, a comparatively new member of a social club, is about to write to Henry Cash, a long-established member of the club and now its treasurer. He is going to suggest that all funds in excess of £100 in the club's current account at the bank should be transferred to a deposit account. Study his thinking as he works out how to tackle this piece of writing. He goes about it in a sensible way, so you will find some useful tips here.

Objective To present the treasurer with such a well-founded and persuasive argument that he will take the advocated action.

Having thought out his objective, Jack Jones considers the other circumstances of the writing situation. Only by taking them into account can he write in such a way that is likely to persuade the treasurer to do what he wants him to do. His choice of contents, form and style must be made in the light of those circumstances.

Contents (i) Facts (drawn from statement of accounts circulated to all club members) about club's present financial position. Only such facts as are relevant to the matter in hand.

(ii) Jack Jones's knowledge that the club is not committed to any heavy expenditure in the near future.

(iii) Rate of interest that the bank will pay for money on deposit.

(iv) Tax status of club. (It is a registered charity.)

Form (i) Letter? Postcard? Informal note? Formal memorandum?

(ii) Postcard rejected at once as being unsuitable in these circumstances. (Too public.) A letter seems the most suitable form, but Jack Jones does not make up his mind before giving the writer/reader relationship full consideration – see later.

Style (i) He is writing about club business, and his message will be 'on the record'. It may well be read out to the club committee at its next meeting, under the agenda heading 'Treasurer's report' or 'Correspondence'.

(ii) Writer/reader relationship. Jack Jones is a newly-joined member: Henry Cash has been a member for a long time and now holds an important office in the club. That office is, in fact, the only reason for Jack Jones to write to him.

(iii) Both the above circumstances make a formal style appropriate.

(iv) Jack Jones's personal knowledge of Henry Cash clinches the argument for a formal style and provides useful hints on which he will act when writing. The treasurer is an elderly man; not pompous, perhaps, but well aware of his standing in the club and of the importance of his official position. Anything chatty or free and easy in the writing would put him off.

Bearing all those circumstances in mind, Jack Jones decides that his message must be in the form of a letter. He has already rejected a postcard as unsuitable (too 'open') for the discussion of financial matters. His knowledge of Henry Cash tells him that an informal note would be resented as too familiar. But a formal memorandum would seem much too stiff and starchy in these circumstances.

Postcard rejected at once as being unsuitable in these circumstances.

He then has to decide whether to begin his letter with 'Dear Sir' or 'Dear Mr Cash'. Since he knows the treasurer (they see each other at meetings and they are, after all, members of the same club) 'Dear Sir' would be inappropriate - so cold and distant as to be discourteous in these circumstances. He chooses to begin 'Dear Mr Cash' and to end 'Yours sincerely'. (If 'Dear Sir' had been appropriate, then the ending would have been 'Yours faithfully'.)

While he is writing, Jack Jones tries to choose his words tactfully. He must not give Henry Cash the impression that he is trying to teach him his business.

Go through that account of Jack Jones's thinking again, noting carefully how he sets about his task. Then read the letter that he wrote (see pp. 73-4). Pay special attention to the order in which he presented the relevant facts and developed his arguments.

Exercise 3

Jane Brown has sent for a jumper and skirt by mail order. When she unpacks the parcel, she finds a jumper of the colour she ordered, but not the size; and she finds a skirt of the size she ordered, but not the colour.

She must now return the garments and ask the suppliers either to replace them with others that meet her requirements, or to refund the money she sent with her order.

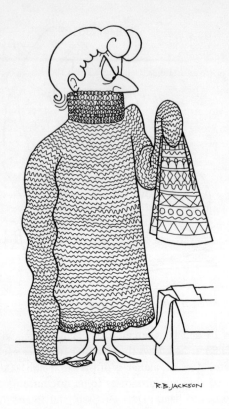

When she unpacks the parcel . . .

Because she sensibly kept the advertisement from which she ordered the goods and made a copy of her order, she can provide all the details needed to clear up the mistake. She will also quote the reference number printed on an 'advice of delivery' slip enclosed in the parcel.

However, she still has to think out the best way of writing the message which she must send with the returned goods.

Her first thought is to write a letter. She makes a start:

Dear Sirs,

JB4a12J310S

When I unpacked the parcel, I discovered that . . .

'That's not crisp enough' she rightly decides. It sounds more like the beginning of a narrative than the opening words of a strictly transactional message. She tries again:

Dear Sirs,

JB4a12J310S

I am returning the jumper and skirt because the jumper is the wrong colour and the skirt is the wrong size.

If you refer to my order dated . . .

'That won't do, either' she thinks. 'It's clear, but it's moving too slowly.' If she continues along those lines, she is going to write quite a long letter.

After those two attempts, Jane Brown begins to question whether a letter is the best form for this message to take. All the circumstances in which it is to be written (reader, occasion, subject matter and purpose – *ROSP*) are cut and dried. Her message must be strictly transactional – impersonal, streamlined, economical. It must make its impact on its reader as swiftly as possible.

'Exactly what have I got to do?' she asks herself. Then she narrows it down to the bare essentials:

1 Tell them why I'm returning the jumper and skirt.
2 Ask for replacements.
3 Ask for my money back if they can't send replacements.
4 Ask them to refund the postage it costs me to return the goods.

She now decides that, in all the circumstances, even a strictly formal letter would be an unnecessarily elaborate way of tackling the job. The conventional courtesies appropriate to a letter, such as a 'salutation' ('Dear Sirs' in this case) and a 'formal close' ('Yours faithfully' in this case) would be superfluous. But, if she writes a letter, she will have to use them.

Having decided, quite rightly, that the situation calls for the clearest, simplest message written in the fewest possible words, she gives up the idea of writing a letter. Instead, she writes a strictly formal business message, making use of headings and numbered sections. (Such a note is usually called a *memorandum*.)

The note that Jane Brown wrote is printed on page 74. Before you read it, write a note of your own that meets all the circumstances of the situation in which she was placed.

But if you do not agree with the decision she took, write a letter instead. Then compare your letter with her note and see which is the better message in the circumstances.

CHAPTER 4

HOW?

Whatever you are writing, *clarity* is the overriding consideration. Your first aim should always be to help your reader to understand what you are writing – and to understand it as quickly and easily as possible.

When you are wondering how to tackle a piece of practical writing, remember this golden rule:

- Set its contents out in a sensible *order* and use *plain* language.

4.1 ORDERLY ARRANGEMENT

Having decided what must be included (what is relevant to the matter in hand – see Sections 3.2 and 3.3) your next job is to arrange the contents in a sensible order. In this context, 'sensible' means *easy to understand*.

- The order of presentation is sensible (easy to understand) when one thing follows another in a *logical* (reasoned) *sequence*.

Different methods of arrangement suit different kinds of writing jobs. According to the particular kind of job you are doing, one or another of the methods described below will help you to set its contents out in a logical sequence.

(a) Parts, stages, steps
Whenever you have to supply information, describe a process, give instructions, or make requests, analyse your subject-matter into its separate parts, stages or steps.

Once you have done that, it is not difficult to arrange the various items in a sensible order, for writing jobs such as these have a natural, common-sense order built into them.

For example, if you are writing a note to a neighbour asking him to collect your newspapers while you are away, this is the common sense sequence:

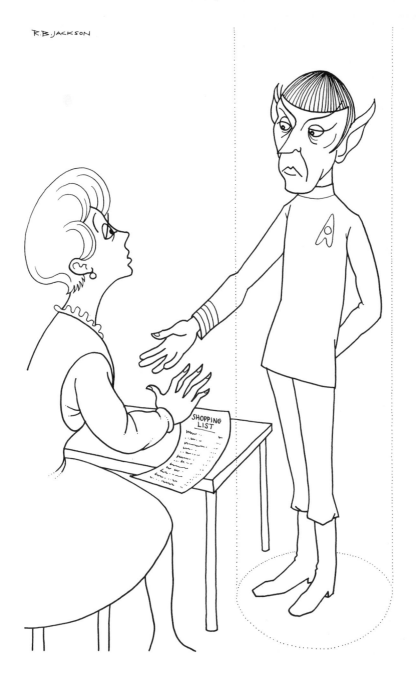

The order of presentation is sensible when one thing follows another in a logical sequence.

1. Tell him what you want.
2. Tell him which newsagent you go to and which paper(s) you have on order there.
3. Tell him when you'll be back. (End, of course, by thanking him. That is an essential courtesy though not, strictly speaking, a stage of the 'request-making' process.)

That is a simple example, but – as the following exercises demonstrate – the parts, stages, steps method works just as well in more complicated situations.

Exercise 1

Miss Green works in the tourist information department of Seatown Borough Council. The Council has just completed the restoration of an Elizabethan merchant's house ('Jeavon's Place') in Seatown High Street. It will be opened to the public at Easter, and Miss Green is preparing an information sheet for visitors.

She has been supplied with a hefty file of facts about the history and architecture of Jeavon's Place from which to select the information most likely to interest visitors. Allowing for eye-catching headings and generous display, she is limited to not more than 450 words of informational text.

She studies the file and selects the material she needs for her purpose. The problem then is how to set it out. It soon becomes clear to her that the material she has selected falls quite naturally into groups, like this:

Having analysed her subject matter into its component parts, she has worked out the basic structure on which she can organise her writing. The contents of the information sheet will be divided into sections, each of which will correspond to one part of the subject matter.

She has not yet reasoned out a logical order of presentation, so her plan is not finished. Asking herself which order will be most helpful to her readers, she finds a commonsense answer: 'They'll see the exterior first, so start with that. Then they'll go into the entrance hall, so describe that next ... and so on.'

Because she has identified the component parts of her subject-matter *and* reasoned out a way of arranging them in a logical sequence, she can now complete her plan, noting as she does so the details to be included in each section.

Turn to pages 74–5, where you will find the final plan that Miss Green worked out. It provides some useful hints on how to plan a piece of informational writing.

Exercise 2

John Smith, a student in his final year at a Sixth Form College, was asked to write a hand-out for first-year students applying for membership of the college music society. When asking him to do the job, the society's chair-person emphasised the need for a clear, brief statement of the procedure that applicants should follow.

Study the hand-out that John Smith wrote. The facts are correct, and it is literate. Even so, you may think that its readers would not have found it very helpful.

THE MUSIC SOCIETY

First-year students wishing to join should note that this is one of the most popular societies in college. It organises a programme of subscription concerts and provides members with other advantages, such as the loan of instruments, books and scores. Applications for membership are dealt with on a strictly first-come, first-served basis (subject to the committee's decisions as to candidates' qualifications), and students should note that the closing date for applications is a fortnight from the first day of this term. The number of applications generally exceeds the number of vacant places, so some evidence of musical aptitude, experience and genuine enthusiasm will be an advantage to applicants. We shall be pleased to welcome new members to the first subscription concert of this term, which will take place at 8 p.m. on Saturday 21 October in College Hall. Forms should be returned promptly. Be sure to fill in all the details asked for, especially those relating to previous musical experience, ample space for which is provided in Part 3 of the form.

Bearing in mind what John Smith was asked to do, say what mistakes you think he made. Ask these questions:

1 Did he include irrelevant material?
2 Did he supply all the information that his readers needed?
3 Did he identify the separate stages of the application procedure and present them in a logical sequence?
4 Did he use more words than were necessary?

In the light of your answers to those questions, write an improved version of that hand-out. Make use of any relevant facts as supplied by John Smith. Add any further information that your readers would need. Then compare your hand-out with the one printed on page 75).

(b) Chronological order

When you are trying to get something done, it helps if you begin at the beginning! That is why a chronological order of presentation is so often the most effective way of organising a piece of transactional writing.

Once you have analysed your subject-matter into its component parts (*always* the essential first step) it is often apparent that they can be arranged in a time sequence. By setting them out in that order, you help your reader to understand the *connection* between one part and another. You are, as we say, making it easy for your reader to 'follow' you.

For example, suppose you are lending your camera to a relative to use on holiday. You start to explain how to load it, but he/she says, 'I'll never remember all that. Write it out for me.' Having written a detailed explanation of how to insert the film leader into the take-up spool slot, you realise that the operation doesn't start there! The first thing to be done is to open the camera back, and that should have been the first item of the instructions you are giving. If you'd organised them in time sequence before you began to write, you'd have begun with what must be done first.

This principle of 'first things first' applies to all practical writing. Often, the first thing is the first *in time*. In some circumstances, however, other

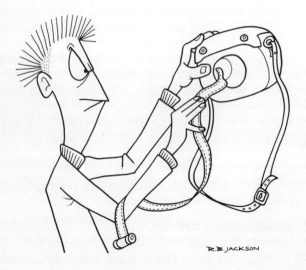

R.B JACKSON

. . . the operation doesn't start there!"

considerations apply, and you must then look for another method of arrangement.

(c) Spatial order

In this context, 'spatial' means *according to space*. So 'spatial order' is an order of presentation based on *where*, rather than (as in chronological order) *when*.

The efficiency of an informational or instructional piece of writing sometimes depends on how clearly it indicates the *position* ('the place in space'!) occupied by each item of its contents. In such circumstances, the reader finds it easier to take in the information or to follow the instructions if the writer groups the various items according to their physical positions. In other words, spatial order is then the logical sequence of presentation.

Exercise 1 in Section 4.1(a) provided an example. Miss Green organised the subject-matter of the information sheet she was writing by grouping the items according to their physical positions. Basing the order of presentation on *where*, she set the information out in a clear, common-sense sequence: exterior before interior; entrance hall and ground-floor rooms before staircase . . . and so on.

(d) Functional order

This is another well-tried method of establishing a clear and readily-comprehensible order of presentation. The various items to be dealt with are grouped by *function* – in other words, by what they *do*, or what they are *used for*.

Exercise 3

Here is an example of the kind of writing job in which the contents are best set out in functional order. An extra telephone is needed for the office in which Janet White works. The office manager tells her to go to the Telecom Shop and inspect what instruments are available within a given price range. 'Write a report on them when you get back,' she adds. 'Let me have it after lunch, so that I can decide today which is best for us.'

Having inspected the instruments carefully and obtained a descriptive leaflet for each, Janet has collected all the necessary information. Her problem now is how to organise the contents of her report. Two considerations are uppermost in her mind:

1　How to make it easy for her reader to take in the information.
2　How to help her reader to use that information to make a good decision.

In all the circumstances, she decides that an order of presentation based on function is best suited to her purposes. If she groups the features of each of the telephones according to what they do, she will help her reader to see the advantages and disadvantages of each. A functional order of presentation will draw meaningful comparisons between one feature and another, because like will be compared with like. (There would be no sense, for instance, in arranging the contents of the report so that the colour of one instrument was set against the shape of another. That would not establish a meaningful comparison, because like would *not* be compared with like.)

Consider that situation and take a close look at some telephones. Do you think that Janet was right to decide on a functional order of presentation? If not, try to find a better way of setting out the report. Then work out a suitable plan of your own before studying the plan on pages 75–6.

Any well-written 'user's manual' (for a camera, washing machine, or car, for example) will repay close study. Its efficiency depends on its writer's skill in setting out the contents in a readily comprehensible sequence. It has a lot to teach you about orderly presentation.

In such a piece of writing, the writer has different jobs to do in different sections of the manual, and the methods of presentation are varied accordingly. Different kinds of order suit different purposes.

The handbook supplied with my typewriter illustrates this point. Its contents are clearly set out, the order of presentation varying to suit whatever purpose is uppermost. For example, in the course of the first two pages, the writer uses each of the methods of arrangement described earlier in this chapter, selecting them carefully to suit the nature of each particular job. Here is an analysis of the contents of those pages and of the order of presentation used in each section.

Section 1
Parts and controls of machine identified. Contents grouped and set out in *spatial* order.
Section 2
Uses of each part and control explained. Contents grouped and set out in *functional* order.
Section 3
Operating instructions given for inserting paper and setting line format. Contents grouped and set out in *chronological* order.

(e) Ascending order/descending order
The methods explained earlier are particularly suited to informational and instructional writing.

When the writer's objective is persuasive, argumentative or motivational (see Section 3.4), one or the other of the methods explained in this section is more suitable.

(i) *Ascending order of importance*
Start with introductory and illustrative items that *lead up to* your main point(s).

This is an effective order of presentation *provided that* you do not spend too much time on less important matters - or place too much emphasis on them - before getting to your main point(s). The danger is that you may distract, puzzle, or bore your reader by taking too long to come to the real nub of the matter in hand.

When it is well done (and that means when you maintain a just proportion between major and minor matters) the *climactic* effect of ascending order helps to put the message across.

(ii) *Descending order of importance*
Start with your main point(s). Then go on to the illustrative and supportive items that reinforce the main point(s) with which you began.

Descending order of importance is very often the common-sense order of presentation. By beginning with what matters most, you get your reader's attention at once.

It is important to avoid a tailing-off (an *anti-climax*) so be careful not to string out the minor items following the main point(s).

Be on guard, too, against repetition. Keep the main point where it belongs - at the beginning - and set it out fully and completely. What follows must be clearly illustrative and supportive - *not* a restatement of the main point(s) in different words.

But with those warnings in mind you will often find that descending order of importance provides an effective structure, enabling you to deal crisply and clearly with the matter in hand.

Generally speaking, this order of presentation is easier to handle than ascending order of importance, which requires a more developed sense of direction and control.

According to circumstances (and especially the nature of your subject-matter and your objective), one or the other of these methods of arrangement will be the more suitable. That is why you must familiarise yourself with both, and practise using them to extend the range of your practical writing skills.

Exercise 4
Study these examples of practical writing, and then answer the questions. Do not look at the answers on page 76 until you have done your best to work out your own.

(a) *Extract from a college librarian's report circulated to all members of the library committee*

Item 3

I recommend the committee to terminate the present provision for overnight borrowing of books from the reference library. Many students ignore their obligation to return reference books by 8.30 a.m. the following day. In consequence, the resources of the reference library are being eroded, to the detriment of the majority of students. I hope to have the committee's full support in bringing this unhappy experiment to an immediate end.

... the resources of the library are being eroded ...

(b) *Extract from the quarterly bulletin of the Northmoor Protection Society*

Membership

Membership has been at roughly its present figure (1760) for the past two years. We could hardly expect to maintain the rapid growth of our first two years, but it is disappointing that we have not made better progress since the society's work and successes have become so widely known.

Losses and gains have been in balance for too long, and your committee believes that we merit a wider response. To that end, we have

conducted an advertising campaign in national and local papers, rein-
forcing this with the carefully-targetted postal distribution of 500
leaflets.

But the society's growth depends ultimately on the recruiting
enthusiasm of individual members, which is why you will find at the
end of this bulletin four detachable membership forms for your own
use. Please distribute them to acquaintances, friends and relatives who
are likely to be sympathetic to our aims.

We are asking you to bring in at least one new member before June,
so that we get a substantial increase in our numbers to support this
summer's campaigning.

(i)   Briefly, and in your own words, describe the main objective of
      each of those writers.
(ii) Identify the sentence or sentences in which that objective is
      expressly stated.
(iii) Describe the order of presentation employed in each piece of
      writing.
(iv) Say, with reasons, why you do or do not think that the order of
      presentation is suited to the writer's subject matter and objective.

4.2 ENDS AND MEANS

Your overriding concern is to help your reader to understand your message
quickly and clearly. Whatever particular form your message takes (memo,
report, note or letter) and whether your objective is to inform, to instruct,
to request, to motivate or to persuade, make sure that the way you write is
not likely to cause delays or misunderstandings.

Section 4.1 suggested methods of arranging your subject matter in an
orderly and readily comprehensible sequence. Chapters 5 and 6 discuss a
matter of equal importance: how to use plain language. Chapter 5 provides
advice on finding the right words. Chapter 6 shows you how to use them
directly, by combining them in clear, uncluttered constructions. Those
two chapters illustrate practical applications of the fundamental principles
on which good transactional writing is based.

Unless you direct your reader's attention to the matter in hand, and
keep it there, you are not likely to get anything done about it. Digressions,
superfluous words and winding sentences are distractions. Your reader
loses the thread and becomes confused, or bored, or irritated.

Never waste time (your reader's and your own) with indirect, long-
winded language. Good writing is disciplined and restrained. Its means are
strictly proportioned to its ends. Allowing for the requirements imposed
on you by different forms and circumstances (for example, it would not
be appropriate to write a formal letter in memo style) apply this basic rule

to all your practical writing: use no more words than are needed to make your meaning instantly clear.

When you are making a journey, the shortest route from starting-point to destination is the straightest line that circumstances permit.

And when you are writing, the shortest route from starting-point (*you*) to destination (*your reader*) is also the straightest line that circumstances permit.

So, whenever you have a piece of practical writing to do, bear this advice in mind:

- Never use more words than are strictly necessary.
- Never use a long word when a shorter one will do just as well.
- Never write a long sentence when a shorter one will do just as well.

FINDING THE RIGHT WORDS

Every practical writing job you have to do (report, letter, summary, memorandum - whatever its particular form) is a test of your ability to use language:

- clearly;
- appropriately;
- concisely.

In so far as your writing has all three of those qualities, your reader will be likely to respond in the way you want, and the transaction you have in hand will be advanced.

In so far as your writing is deficient in any of those qualities, your reader will be unable or unwilling to respond in the way you want. If it is not clear, your reader will misunderstand you. If it is not appropriate, your reader will be put off and, therefore, not readily co-operative. If it is not concise, your reader will be irritated and/or confused - distracted from the matter in hand.

Told that you cannot write well (that is, clearly, appropriately and concisely) unless you find the right words, you would probably reply, 'Of course not. That's obvious!'

It may be obvious, but we do not take nearly enough trouble to do so. It is not easy to make the required mental effort, and we are all inclined to dodge the task. We take the easy way out, using the first words that come to mind. Or, more conscientiously, we take a little trouble, and make do with words that are 'nearly right'. Then we are disappointed - sometimes offended - when our reader does not understand or reacts badly to what we have written.

Nobody can relieve you of the hard work of finding the right words, but there are ways of approaching the job that will help you to tackle it successfully.

Finding the right words.

5.1 **CLEAR LANGUAGE**

We are all so used to writing words for other people to read that we rarely stop to consider exactly what it is that we are doing; and very rarely indeed do we ask ourselves how it works.

Think about it. On a sheet of paper you are making marks (writing words) which will transfer thoughts, information, requests, commands, instructions - whatever it is - from your mind into the mind of another person. (That is, if you make the *right* marks on the sheet of paper!)

How is it done? You can, of course, 'explain' it by saying, 'I can write, and the other person can read.' But that doesn't really explain anything.

You need a better explanation than that. If you understand how words work, you will be more likely to use them clearly.

(a) **Words and their meanings**

When drivers see a red light at a road junction, they know what it means. How? By recognising that it stands for (represents or symbolises) this command: 'You must bring your vehicle to a halt at this junction, and you must not proceed until the light changes to green.' The red light is a *symbol*.

When drivers see the word STOP painted on the road, they know what it means. How? By recognising that it represents (or *symbolises*) this command: 'You must bring your vehicle to a halt at this junction, and you must not proceed until you are sure that the road is clear.' The word STOP is a *symbol*.

That is an accurate illustration of how words work. They represent (*symbolise*) something.

- The meaning of a word is what it represents. You know its meaning when you recognise what it represents.

The writing/reading process can be broken down into its successive stages, like this:

1 You have 'things' in your mind that you want to transfer into the mind of your reader.
2 You find words to represent those 'things' in your mind.
3 You write the words down.
4 Your reader sees the words you have written.
5 Your reader recognises the 'things' that your words represent.

That is how the words you write carry 'things' from your mind into your reader's mind.

For the writing/reading process to work successfully, two conditions are essential:

1 The words you choose must be clear, accurate representations of the 'things' you want to pass on.
2 Your reader's 'vocabulary' must enable him/her to recognise the 'things' that your words represent.

If your choice of words is bad, or if your reader's vocabulary is inadequate, one or more of the following will result:

1 The 'things' you have in mind will *not* be transferred into your reader's mind.
2 Only *some* of the 'things' you have in mind will be transferred into your reader's mind.
3 The 'things' that are transferred into your reader's mind will be *different from* the 'things' that were in your mind.

(b) Concepts

In explaining how words work, the term 'things' has been used in the key statements. For example: 'Words represent *things*' and 'Words transfer *things* from the writer's mind into the reader's mind'.

That is a way of putting it with which we are familiar. Expressions such as 'There are things I must tell you' are in daily use.

But the 'things' that words represent may be of very different kinds. To give a few examples: the word 'chair' represents an article of furniture - a *concrete* (that is, a 'real') 'thing'. The word 'honesty' represents a moral quality - an *abstract* 'thing'. (It is just as 'real' a 'thing' as *chair* but it has no *physical* existence.) The 'thing' that the word 'depart' represents is an action. The 'thing' that the word 'promptly' represents is the manner in which an action is performed. The 'thing' that the word 'over' represents is a spatial position.

Different as they may be, the 'things' that a writer's words represent always have one all-important feature in common. They are 'mental pictures' or 'models' that the writer has in mind.

To these 'mental pictures' the term *concepts* is generally applied.

So, when you write the *word* 'chair' you are writing it to represent the *concept* 'chair'; and you write the word in order to transfer that concept into your reader's mind.

When you write the *word* 'honesty' you are writing it to represent the *concept* 'honesty'; and you write the word in order to transfer that concept into your reader's mind.

Some concepts can be transferred with little difficulty and with little risk of confusion. For example, the concept represented by the word 'telephone' will generally pass clearly and readily from the writer's mind into the reader's.

Other concepts – especially 'abstractions' – are difficult to put over. For example, the concept that the word 'liberty' represents to the writer may be very different from the concept that it represents to the reader.

That is why you have to be so careful when you are choosing your words. Ask yourself these two questions:

1 Do these words clearly and accurately represent the concepts that I want to transfer into my reader's mind?
2 Are they likely to represent to my reader the *same* concepts that they represent to me?

The rest of this chapter suggests ways in which you can ensure that the answer to both of those questions is 'Yes'.

Note

Having studied those explanations, you know how words work, so there is now no objection to using the familiar terms: 'mean', 'meaning', 'understand', 'understanding'. They are convenient and perfectly acceptable terms – *so long as you understand what they mean*!

Compare these two statements:

A. I understand this writer's meaning.
B. I recognise the concepts that are represented by the words this writer has used.

A is a quicker way of expressing *B*. It is the everyday, common-sense way of putting it. But don't forget that *A* is 'shorthand' for *B*. *A* is convenient. *B* provides a full and accurate statement of what *A* means.

The consequences of bad (inaccurate and/or unclear) choice of words can now be restated in the familiar terms.

If your wording is bad, one or more of the following will be the result:

1 Your reader will not understand your meaning *at all*.
2 Your reader will *partly* understand your meaning.
3 Your reader will *think* that he/she understands your meaning but will, in fact, understand something *different* from what you intended.

Exercise 1

This word game illustrates two facts:

1 that words represent 'things in the mind' – concepts;
2 that we know what words mean when we recognise the concepts that they represent.

Your reader will . . . understand something different from what you intended.

We all know the meaning of the word *tape*. Now rearrange its letters to make the word *peat*. Again, we all know what it means. Yet another rearrangement of the letters makes the word *pate*. Most of us know what it means.

Test your knowledge of the meaning of all three words by using them in sentences.

Now rearrange the letters yet again to make the 'word' *atep*. Do you know what it means? (Don't try to look it up in a dictionary – you won't find it.) You will probably say, 'It doesn't mean anything' or, 'It isn't a word'. Yet it has the same letters as *tape*, *peat* and *pate*, and you know what they mean.

Think out the answers to these questions:

1 Why don't you know what *atep* means?
2 What do you mean when you say, 'It isn't a word.'?

Now try to invent some more 'non-words', using the tape/peat/pate/ atep method. To start with, see what you can do with *rope*, *heat* and *trap*. Then try some bigger words.

(c) Words and their contexts

Bear these two facts in mind when you are trying to find the right words:

1 Most words can represent more than one concept. (To put it in familiar everyday terms: most words can have more than one meaning.)

2 Different words can represent the same or nearly the same concept. (To put it in familiar everyday terms: different words can have the same or nearly the same meaning.)

For example:

1 The word 'house' can represent any of the following concepts:
  (i)   a building for human habitation;
  (ii) a building in which a legislative body (members of parliament, senators, representatives, and so on) meets;
  (iii) the legislative body itself – as in 'After a stormy debate, the House rose at midnight.';
  (iv) a building in which animals are kept or goods are stored.
  (That is by no means a complete list of all the meanings that the word 'house' can have.)
2 The concept *house* can be represented by any of the following words:
  (i)   dwelling;
  (ii) cottage;
  (iii) abode;
  (iv) mansion;
  (v)   habitation;
  (vi) residence.
  (That is by no means a complete list of all the words that can mean *house*.)

Note the use of *can* in the above statements and examples: 'Most words *can* have more than one meaning.'/'Different words *can* have the same meaning.'/'The word "house" *can* mean "a family".' – and so on.

The word 'house' *can* mean 'a family', but it does *not* mean 'a family' in this sentence: 'We sold our house the following year, when prices had risen a little.' There, it means 'a building for human habitation'.

The words 'house', 'habitation', 'mansion' *can* all be used to represent the concept *a building for human habitation*, but none of them would be a suitable choice to fill the gap in this sentence: 'Guided tours of Stratford generally include a visit to Anne Hathaway's – in their itinerary.' The word 'cottage' is usually selected to represent the concept of that particular building for human habitation; and that is the word the reader would expect to see. None of the other 'house words' would be recognised as an appropriate choice *in that context*.

To sum up:

● A word *can* have several different meanings. Which of those meanings it *does* have is determined by *the context in which it is used.*

● Several different words *can* mean the same or nearly the same thing. Which of those words is the *right* choice is determined by *the context in which it is used.*

Exercise 2

Choose three words and list for each two different meanings that it can have. Use each word in two sentences, bringing out those two different meanings (six sentences in all).

Exercise 3

Choose three different words having the same or nearly the same meaning. Write three sentences in each of which *one* of those words is the right choice where the other two would not be.

Exercise 4

(Answers on page 76) Select the right word to fill the gap in each of the following sentences. If none of the suggested words seems right, try to think of one that provides exactly the right meaning in the context of the sentence.

(i) Please send marked-up photocopies of any pages on which printer's errors occur, so that — can be made in any future reprint. (additions - substitutions - corrections - alterations)

(ii) In our opinion, your client's — to settle this claim within a month is a reasonable compromise in this situation, and we have advised our client accordingly. (promise - pledge - undertaking - guarantee)

(iii) By adopting a — strategy, we have achieved a more than satisfactory return on our invested funds in a dangerously volatile market. (wise - prudent - cautious - sober - watchful)

(iv) If the new consultative work groups function as planned, managers will be able to — employees' practical suggestions much more speedily. (employ - utilise - implement - exploit)

(v) Unexpected problems in the — of washers for our new range of compressors set us back, but we are now producing these basic components in sufficient numbers to meet the needs of the assembly line. (handicraft - manufacture - craftsmanship - workmanship)

(d) Sense of audience

When choosing your words and framing the sentences in which you use them, you should, as far as possible, place every key word and expression in a context that makes its intended meaning clear to your reader.

Sometimes, however, the particular circumstances in which you are writing - circumstances of readership, of occasion, of subject matter, of purpose - put special difficulties in your way. You cannot always rely on the immediate context to make your meaning fully clear. There will be times when your reader can understand the literal meaning of your words without grasping their special senses and implications.

For example, when Janet White was writing her report on the telephones she had inspected, she made use of technical terms, such as 'memory storage and retrieval system (see page 76). She was writing the report for her office manager to read, so she was entitled to expect that particular reader to understand those 'special sense' terms. Explanation would have been superfluous - a waste of her time and that of her reader. It would also have been tactless, appearing to suggest that the office manager did not understand terms that she certainly ought to have been able to understand.

But suppose Janet White had been writing for another reader - a friend, say, who wanted advice on which telephone to buy, and who lacked the special knowledge that the office manager possessed. In that situation, Janet could not expect her reader to understand the 'special sense' terms without help. To make their meaning clear, she might include the necessary explanations in the sentences in which she used the technical ('special sense') terms. Or, if that made for long and difficult sentences, she would write additional sentences to explain them.

Earlier discussions of content and style stressed the importance of giving due weight to particular circumstances of readership, occasion, subject matter and purpose. Together, those circumstances constitute what is called 'the context of situation' - a useful 'shorthand' expression to describe the network of circumstances within which you are writing.

Your awareness of the context of situation - and especially your awareness of the reader for whom you are writing - plays a crucial part in guiding you to a successful choice of words.

Exercise 5

Study this example of what happens when a writer's *sense of audience* is faulty.

Jim Miller has turned his hobby of making model aircraft into a one-man business. So far, his sales have been made to trade customers, but he has recently advertised in a modellers' magazine, hoping to sell to private customers as well. Soon, his first order from a private collector arrives. Jim packs up the model, enclosing with it the bill, at the bottom of which he writes: 'Prompt payment entitles customers to a 2 per cent discount.'

What Jim has overlooked is the fact that the words he has used will not make clear to this particular reader (a private customer) exactly what he/she must do to be entitled to the discount. Does 'prompt payment' mean 'by return' - or 'within a week' - or 'within 28 days'?

Whereas Jim's trade customers know what the words 'prompt payment' mean (because they are familiar with the context of situation in which Jim has used the words), Jim's private customers will not understand them clearly (because they are not familiar with the context of situation in which Jim has used the words). They will understand the *literal* meaning

What happens when your sense of audience is faulty.

of the words 'prompt payment', of course; but they will *not* understand their implications. Jim's message will not get through clearly and quickly.

A sharper sense of audience would have suggested a clearer wording – something like this: 'Prompt payment (i.e. within 7 days) entitles customers to a 2 per cent discount'.

Obviously, Jim Miller could have explained 'prompt payment' as meaning 'within 28 days' (or whatever period he has decided on). The point is that he should have realised that *this* kind of reader needed an explanation.

Don't imagine that Jim Miller was stupid or unusually careless. The mistake he made is very common. Take a close look at recent examples of your own practical writing and apply these tests to what you have written:

1 In *this* context of situation, could I reasonably expect *this* reader to understand all my words in the way that I intended them to be understood?
2 Did I fail to realise that I was using some of these words in a *special sense* and that I ought to have made that special sense clear to my reader?

Only by putting yourself in your reader's place (see Chapter 2) when you are choosing your words can you avoid misunderstandings.

- Wording that would be clear to one kind of reader may be hard - even impossible - for another kind of reader to understand. Sense of audience is the key to successful word choice.

(e) Three useful techniques

As stated in the previous section, it is not always necessary (or tactful) to explain the meaning of technical terms or of words used in a special sense. You have to decide whether or not to explain them in the light of what you know - or can reasonably assume - about your reader's knowledge of the matter in hand.

Play safe. Whenever you feel that there is even a slight risk of being misunderstood, find a way of making sure that your reader knows what you mean.

Try not to be clumsy or long-winded about it. Your explanations should be brief. If you have to write long explanatory sentences to get your message across, you have chosen the wrong words in the first place.

There are three well-tried techniques that can be employed:

1 Make the meaning clear by using the word or term *in a context that illustrates its meaning.*
2 Provide an immediate *explicit explanation*, either in a parenthesis or in a brief sentence, as soon as you have used the word or term.
3 Provide a *definition* before you use the word or term.

The following three examples show you how to use each of those explanatory techniques.

1. Contextual illustration of meaning (from a letter written by a parent to a university student)

I can't complete the grant application form until I know what you earned during vacations in the last tax year, so let me have a note of your earnings between 6 April last year and 5 April this year.

2. Immediate explicit explanation (from a letter written by an accountant to a client)

Please complete the enclosed statement of income form for the tax year just ended (i.e. from 6 April 1988 to 5 April 1989) and return it to me as soon as possible.

3. Preliminary definition (from the first article in a series entitled 'Taxation Made Simple')

The term 'tax year' means the twelve-month period beginning on 6 April in one year and ending on 5 April in the next.

In most cases, you will find that one or another of those three methods provides a clear, economical way of getting your meaning across.

5.2 **APPROPRIATE LANGUAGE**

Clarity is always of first importance, but it is not the sole consideration. Your wording must be clear *and appropriate*. Compare these two pieces of writing. Each is clearly worded, and each is appropriately worded – but it would not do to put them in the wrong envelopes!

A Note from head of Brown & Co's legal department to chief assistant
Here's Nitpick & Pore's latest letter – same old stuff! I'm fed up with them, and I'm not prepared to waste any more time. Get a reply off today and try to shut them up.

B Extract from chief Assistant's letter to Messrs Nitpick & Pore
Your letter of 5 September does not contain any information with which we were unfamiliar when we wrote to you on 4 August. Consequently, we do not think that we can be of any further help to you in this matter.

As has been emphasised earlier (and as the example just given demonstrates), the right wording is that which is suited to a particular reader, a particular occasion, a particular subject and a particular purpose. What is appropriate in one set of circumstances is not appropriate in another.

If you have followed the arguments of this book so far, you will not need to have that point elaborated now. There are, however, some recurrent problems that can usefully be singled out for special attention.

(a) Formality

Because practical writing is concerned with 'official' matters – with 'business to be done' – its language is formal. Even when you are writing about matters the outcome of which affects you personally (when applying for a job, for example, or when advancing arguments for or against a course of action or policy) you should avoid the informalities that are appropriate to personal or creative writing.

However, as you saw in Chapters 2 and 3, good style is a matter of striking the right note – of achieving the right *tone*. Rigid formality sounds stiff and starchy, and that is not the impression you want your writing to make on your reader.

You have to look for a middle way between an excessively formal and an informal style, approaching each piece of practical writing like this:

- What is the appropriate *degree of formality* in *these* circumstances?

Different words may be available to represent the same or nearly the same concept. To make a good choice, you must consider not only the particular *shade of meaning* each of those words would carry in the context

You have to look for a middle way between an excessively formal and an informal style.

in which you are thinking of using it. You must also consider whether it would maintain the particular *degree of formality* you are trying to establish (see Section 3.1).

For example, here are some word pairs: vendor/seller; purchase/buy; reside/live; identical/same; admonish/warn; advocate/recommend. Which word is 'right'? That depends very largely on the degree of formality appropriate to the situation in which it is used.

Consider the vendor/seller alternative as an illustration of the point. In some circumstances, 'vendor' would be an inappropriate choice. It would strike your reader as over-formal - certainly stiff, and probably pompous.

But if you are writing to a lawyer or an estate agent, 'vendor' is the appropriate choice. In *that* context of situation 'vendor' is not an over-formal word. It is the expected word: the correct 'technical term'. And in those circumstances, it maintains the degree of formality appropriate to the particular circumstances in whch you are writing.

The problem is not restricted to the choice of individual words. It is present whenever different ways of expressing the same idea occur to you. In choosing between this phrase and that, between this sentence and that, you must consider which maintains the intended *tone* of your writing.

Apply this test: 'Is this way of putting it too formal or not sufficiently formal to "chime in" with the rest of my writing?'

Exercise 6 *(Answers on page 76)*

Here are two different wordings of the same statement:

1 It's a pity we don't see eye to eye about how much I'll be out of pocket if I go ahead with my bright idea.
2 I regret that we disagree in our estimates of the expense of my project.

Consider each as being appropriate/inappropriate to these two contexts of situation:

A A letter from you to a close friend.
B A letter from you to your bank manager.

Now decide which of the following statements are true:
 (i) 1 is appropriate to *B*.
 (ii) 2 is appropriate to *A*.
 (iii) 1 is inappropriate to *B*.
 (iv) 2 is inappropriate to *A*.
 (v) 1 is appropriate to *A*.
 (vi) 2 is appropriate to *B*.

(b) Objectivity

Good practical writing is plain and matter-of-fact – without frills, as we say. It gets to the point quickly, stays with it (no digressions) and deals with it briefly and clearly.

Writing that has those qualities is often, and approvingly, described as 'business-like'. That description may seem rather flat and unenthusiastic, but if you think about it, you will realise that it is high praise. A business-like way of writing *must* be the best way of handling a transaction.

Words can be used in two different ways: either to make precise statements, or to suggest feelings and attitudes. Business-like writing relies on statement, not on suggestion.

Whether your main purpose is to inform, to instruct, to convince, or to motivate your reader, you are writing about practical matters. Your 'raw material' is *factual*, and you must present it *objectively*.

- Only by choosing words that carry plain, objective meanings can you write in a business-like way.

Think of it like this. Words can be used primarily as 'labels' to identify the 'thing' (the concept) that they represent. Or they can be used primarily as 'signals' to transmit feelings and attitudes associated with the 'thing' (the concept) that they represent.

When a word is used as an 'evocative signal', the reader's attention is concentrated on its *subjective* meaning – on the feelings and attitudes associated with the 'thing' for which the word stands. The 'thing' itself is of secondary importance.

The imaginative power of creative writing – poetry, drama, prose fiction – is very largely derived from the evocative properties of words. The success of your own personal writing will often depend on a skilful use of 'signalling' words to convey your feelings and attitudes.

But only precise, objective language is appropriate in practical writing, for there your aim must always be to pin the meaning down as plainly, directly and exactly as you can.

That is why it is, as a rule, a mistake to use words in a figurative sense. Figurative language works by suggestion and not by statement. Its *nuances* can be misconstrued. When you use a word literally, you are concentrating your reader's attention on one fixed and definite meaning. When you use a word figuratively, you are inviting your reader to 'tune in' to a secondary meaning (or meanings) with which various feelings and attitudes are (or may be) associated. When factual accuracy and objective presentation are your principal aims, figurative language opens up too large an area of potential misunderstanding. Nor is figurative language compatible with the cool, restrained tone appropriate to practical writing.

For example, 'inexperienced' (literal and objective) is preferable to 'green' (figurative and subjective). It is not so colourful, but colourful language is not what you are after! 'Inexperienced' is precisely restricted to one meaning, whereas 'green', though it *can* simply mean 'inexperienced' *may* suggest associated attitudes of a pejorative nature.

A written report that refers to an employee as 'inexperienced' makes an objective – an emotionally neutral – comment. But in that context 'green' may be misconstrued, for it is not emotionally neutral. It is, as we say, 'loaded'. It *could* be taken to suggest personal deficiencies in the employee, even though the writer did not intend to make any such suggestions.

For similar reasons, 'rosy' would not be an appropriate alternative for 'optimistic' in this context: 'The directors' optimistic forecast of next year's results is based on recent and favourable developments in the terms of trade.' Substitute 'rosy' for 'optimistic', and the objectivity of the statement is impaired. 'Rosy' *might* be taken to mean 'optimistic' or 'hopeful', but it *could* be taken as suggesting an over-optimistic attitude – a sanguine assumption of better times to come.

Those are just two examples of the kinds of risks you always run if you choose words that work by suggestion rather than by statement. You cannot be sure that your reader will interpret them as you intend. They may well trigger off feelings and attitudes in your reader's mind that you had no intention of suggesting. You are not in control, because you cannot confine your reader's attention to the exact area of understanding that *you* have in mind.

R.B.JACKSON

'Green' may be misconstrued.

Writers whose purpose it is to manipulate opinion - advertisers, politicians, some journalists, 'public relations' practitioners in general - get their results by using loaded language. You can learn a lot from them about how *not* to use words in your practical writing.

The following exercise is based on five extracts from writing that exploits (or tries to exploit) the reader's suggestibility. Your own daily reading will provide plenty more examples for further practice along the lines set out.

Exercise 7 *(Suggested answers on page 77)*

In so far as you can discover it, try to express the factual meaning of each of these extracts in precise, objective language. (For example: *Take personal advantage of our abundant credit facilities on painlessly easy terms* really means: 'Borrow money from us. We have plenty to lend, and we do not charge more than the going rate of interest.'

(i) Delighted housewives stampede to pay tribute to Rosedrop's magic conquest of distasteful odours.

(ii) Let me be very clear indeed that our searching analysis of our opponents' starry-eyed proposals has unmasked a deeply burrowing worm of heartless deception at their very core.

(iii) Your treasured heirlooms, lovingly crafted in wood by workers of yesterday and today, deserve the gentle, caring cleansing power of Wixwax.

(iv) It is a long time since we have been so confident of a new investment opportunity. We are, therefore, particularly pleased to be able to make this exclusive offer to you on exceptionally favourable terms. But hurry! Our special 1 per cent bonus applies only to those far-sighted investors who mail the application form to reach us by 1 April. This new issue is authorised by the internationally famous house of Richkwik and Partners, whose managed funds have achieved an average annual capital appreciation of 26.5 per cent over the past two years. Can you afford to miss out this time?

(v) Chair*person*! What utter drivel! Chair*man* was good enough for our fathers - and our mothers, too! But tinkering with the language is the stock-in-trade of all trendy pedlars of loony notions. Those same self-styled 'idealists' have forced us to wear seat belts. They'd like to stop us smoking. And now they intend to rob us of our vigorous, manly words.

5.3 CONCISE LANGUAGE

Just as superfluous weight is bad for your health, superfluous words are bad for your writing. Wordiness - *verbosity* - clogs written messages with verbal 'fat'.

The advice on choosing words set out in Sections 5.1 and 5.2 should provide you with adequate defences against verbosity. Plain, business-like writing has no room for superfluous words.

Unfortunately, you will often be under pressure to imitate bad examples, for (judging by much official/business writing) there is a widespread and woolly-minded notion that a crisp, brief style is 'undignified'. A lot of people try to make their writing (and, therefore, themselves) seem *important* by puffing it out.

That is a silly and damaging fault. It is silly because, so far from making them seem important, it makes them seem pretentious and pompous. It is damaging because the presence of unnecessary words obscures the sense of the others.

Even though you may have no intention of puffing out the style of your writing, some verbose habits are so prevalent that you can be infected by them without recognising that you have caught the disease. Nor are you likely to pick up just one of these bad habits. Get into one, and the others will follow.

Puffing it out.

(a) Circumlocution

Circumlocutions are roundabout expressions, and they are used for one or more of the following purposes:

1 to inflate the writer's importance;
2 to conceal the facts;
3 to be in the fashion.

Study this list of circumlocutory tricks, and whenever you feel tempted to use any of them – *don't*!

1 *Unnecessary use of passives*
   Passive constructions are longer and less direct than active constructions. Used unnecessarily, they drain the life out of writing. (See also Section 6.1 [4].)

2 *Unnecessary use of negatives*
   This risk often goes hand-in-hand with unnecessary passives and impersonal formulas, as in 'It is not much to be feared that . . .' and 'There would seem to be a not uncommon belief that . . .'. At best, unnecessary negatives make hesitant understatements. At worst, they seem like mealy-mouthed evasions. Plain, direct, positive statements are always preferable.

3 *Preference for abstract words*
   This is a very common feature of much official and business writing. Striving to be 'important' and 'dignified', writers plaster their messages with polysyllabic abstract words. Plain, direct, *concrete* language is always clearer and quicker, and makes a much more favourable impression on the reader.

4 *Use of stock formulas*
   Plain, direct writing does not come by chance. You have to take trouble and you will often be tempted to dodge the effort by taking a ready-made expression off the shelf. When you fall back on stock language, it is a sign that you cannot be bothered to think. Unless you look for the words *you* need for *your* particular purpose, you cannot complain if your reader gives scant attention to your message.

   A list of some stock expressions commonly used by lazy writers is printed below. Whenever you are about to use any of them, think hard and change your mind, for they will lead you into a verbal quagmire.

   Verbal traps: in/with regard to; in the event that; in the case/instance of; in relation to; in connection with; as to; in respect of; in the majority of; in a position to; will take steps to; it should be noted that; under active consideration; a crisis (or any other) situation.
   There are others, too, and those listed above may appear in slight disguises – for example, 'in respect of' and 'with respect to' are used

A verbal quagmire.

interchangeably. The same objection applies to them all: they are time-wasting and imprecise. Their meaning can be more clearly expressed in one word. For example, 'in the majority of' means *most*; 'in connection with' means *about*.

Exercise 8 *(Suggested answers on p. 77)*

Try to reword these passages concisely and actively, without altering their meaning:

(i) Customers are advised that accounts are rendered monthly and that settlement within 14 days is stipulated by the terms under which business is conducted.

Note Passive constructions *and* inflated language ('advised that'/ 'rendered').

(ii) There would undoubtedly seem to be several important regulations that have been ignored when this application was granted by the planning subcommittee.

Note Try to avoid impersonal introductory expressions such as *There would . . . /There is . . . /It would . . . /It is . . . .* Where you must use them, be on your guard, for they will often trap you into clumsy and unnecessary passives, as in that piece of writing.

Notice the verbiage, too (see Section 5.3[b]). For instance, why write 'important regulations'? In this context, regulations *are* important, so the adjective is superfluous. Again, 'undoubtedly seem to be' is a long-winded and contradictory expression. Its meaning is obscure. Were the regulations ignored, or did they only *seem* to be ignored?

The passage is an example of lazy thinking and slack writing. Cut out the stale 'playsafe formulas' to turn it into a vigorous, active statement.

Exercise 9 *(Suggested answers on p. 77)*

Find a positive, concise rewording for each of these two pieces of writing:

(i) It has proved to be a matter of not inconsiderable difficulty to have the registration of our brand name permitted by the panel.

(ii) We were well aware that it was not to be anticipated that our latest proposals would be met by the union representatives with anything less than a hostile attitude.

Exercise 10 *(Suggested answers on p. 77)*

Cut out all unnecessary abstract words (for example, 'availability', 'eventualisation') and turn these two passages of 'gobbledegook' into plain, direct English:

(i) We have queried our subcontractors concerning the delay in the immediate availability of our supply of door locks.

(ii) The possible eventualisation of redundancy is creating an anxiety situation among our work-force on the shop floor and at management level.

Exercise 11

Look critically at any practical writing that you have had to read recently and at any practical writing that you have had to do. If it contains any of the 'formula expressions' listed above (or any others of the same kind) find concise substitutes. I have a typical example in front of me now. It comes from a letter written to me by a mail order firm:

This is to inform you that your adverse observations with respect to the articles that have been supplied to you have been noted and are under active consideration by our quality control supervisor.

Translated into concise, direct language, that means:

> Our quality control supervisor is considering your complaints about the articles we supplied.

(b) Verbiage: a summing up

Verbiage is best described as 'verbal garbage'. It is an accumulation of rubbish piled up whenever words are used without necessity and without adding much (if anything) to meaning.

All circumlocution is verbiage. The bad habits discussed in the previous section are typical of the flatulent way of writing that many people adopt when they have practical matters to transact. Just when they ought to be most business-like, they pad out their writing with superfluous words.

Be sparing. The shortest way of expressing your meaning is usually the best. Go through your first draft, cutting out every word that is not strictly necessary. Good gardeners prune excessive growth that spoils the shape of a plant and can, if left, kill it. Good writers prune verbose expressions for the same reasons.

Mistakes that are the result of sheer carelessness will not get past an alert reviser. Keep these two pieces of advice in mind, and you will cut out some of the commonest and most elementary forms of verbiage.

1 Look out for unnecessary prepositions. For example: 'reverse *back*'/'advance *forward*'. In what other directions *can* one reverse or advance? So, too: 'reply *back*'. Again, why write 'check up on'? Why not simply 'check'?
2 Look out for unnecessary adjectives and adverbs. For example, the word *actual* adds nothing to the meaning of this statement: 'The actual facts are not in dispute.' The word *definitely* is superfluous here: 'I shall definitely leave on Tuesday.' Again, a thoughtful writer would reject the first three of these four wordings: (i) 'We sincerely and honestly believe that this is a fair offer.' (ii) 'We sincerely believe that this is a fair offer.' (iii) 'We honestly believe that this is a fair offer.' (iv) 'We believe that this is a fair offer.'

But verbiage is not always confined to the isolated trouble spots just mentioned, where it can easily be recognised and eradicated. It has a nasty creeping habit of spreading from phrase to phrase and from sentence to sentence. Watch it! The moment you forget that direct constructions and concise language are the best ways of getting your message across, you are in danger. And once you lower your guard, verbiage is likely to take over.

I am sure you could never write as badly as the people quoted in this next exercise. Even so, it will do you good to study their mistakes and to work out exactly where and why they went wrong.

Creeping verbiage.

Exercise 12 *(Suggested answers on page 77)*

Rewrite these passages, cutting out all verbiage while retaining the intended sense.

(i) The course stewards in charge of the course, in view of the ground conditions consequent upon the prolonged continuation of frosty weather factors, have decided upon a cancellation of the race meeting that was to have taken place at this racecourse today.

(ii) The exporting situation that has developed for several firms in the region now in question virtually guarantees a reversal away from the previously obtaining adverse trends and directions which occasioned serious and harmful losses in the area of overseas export markets.

CHAPTER 6

GETTING A MOVE ON

We write (and read) practical messages – notes, memos, reports, letters – because we *have* to. Their sole purpose is to be *useful*: to carry forward some piece of business, some working matter, in which both writer and reader are involved. We write, and our reader reads, for strictly utilitarian purposes. The criterion of success is the business-like manner in which the writing is done.

It is essential not to waste time. Subject to the overriding importance of clarity, the speed with which your message gets across is the measure of your writing skill. You are much less likely to carry practical matters forward if you keep your reader hanging about!

You have seen already (in Chapter 5) that concise language makes for both clarity and speed. Choosing individual words, however, is only one part of a writer's job. Words have to be *used* – put together in meaningful groups. Clear, quick-moving writing requires a lot of constructional skill. Words must be built into straightforward, concise sentences. Sentences must be grouped in short, logical paragraphs.

6.1 SENTENCES

1. *Keep them short*
   Short sentences hold the reader's attention. They are quicker and easier to read than long ones, and they are clearer. Keep this rule of thumb in mind: if a sentence contains more than 20 words, it's too long.

2. *Keep them simple*
   Avoid complicated sentences. For the purposes of practical writing, simple sentences are more efficient than complex sentences. (A complex sentence contains at least one dependent clause.) Apply that advice sensibly. The contents of two or three simple sentences can sometimes

be condensed into one *short* complex sentence, saving time and without loss of meaning. It is when clause is piled on clause that efficiency falls off.

Compare these two versions of the same operational instruction. *A* is long-winded and foggy. It consists of one long complex sentence containing 52 words. *B* is crisp and readily comprehensible. It consists of four simple sentences, followed by one short complex sentence. The longest sentence (the last) contains 14 words.

A

The carriage locking pin (1), which is held in place by the knurled thumb wheel (2), should always be released before the mains switch (3) is turned to 'ON' to avoid the risk of damage to the carriage drive which can result from a surge of power when the carriage is in the locked position.

B

The carriage locking pin (1) is held in place by the knurled thumb wheel (2). Release the pin by turning the thumb wheel. Then turn the mains switch (3) to the 'ON' position. Do not switch the current on before releasing the carriage. If the carriage is locked, a sudden surge of power may damage the drive.

3. *Keep them taut*

In any sentence, the subject and its verb make the main statement. Keep them close together. If you wedge words in between the subject and its verb, the sentence is slack. Your reader has to search for the main statement, instead of seeing it bold and clear at once.

Nor should you allow the verb to get separated from its object (or its complement). The meaning of the verb is carried over to its object (or completed by its complement). If you do not link them closely, you loosen the sentence structure.

Similarly, place adjectives and adjective phrases as close as possible to their nouns. Place adverbs and adverb phrases as close as possible to their verbs.

Keep this rule in mind: 'Words that *mean together* must *go together.*'

Compare the two sentences which follow. *A* breaks the rule. It is slack and slow. *B* obeys the rule. It is taut and quick.

A

This candidate, in present circumstances, would be, though highly qualified, an unsuitable appointment.

An unsuitable appointment in present circumstances.

B

Though highly qualified, this candidate would be an unsuitable appointment in present circumstances.

4. *Use active verbs whenever possible (see also Section 5.3(a))*
   There's nothing 'wrong' in using the passive voice. Quite often, the sense of what you are writing demands it. It is the unnecessary use of passives that makes practical writing (or any other kind of writing) cumbersome. It is a common fault because people seem to imagine that active verbs are 'undignified' – not 'important' enough in official and business writing. It is infectious nonsense.

   Look at these two pieces of writing. Notice how much more clearly and quickly the second gets it meaning across.

A

You are informed that your letter has been forwarded by this department to the chairperson of the highways sub-committee to which responsibility for preliminary discussion concerning highways matters has been delegated by the council, and you are advised that it will come under active consideration by that body as an item to be treated as requiring immediate and urgent attention.

B

We have sent your letter to the chairperson of the highways sub-committee for immediate attention.

A's preference for passives ('are informed that'/'has been forwarded'/'has been delegated'/'are advised that') is symptomatic of an addiction to circumlocution and stock expressions. These faults generally go together.

By using an active verb and cutting out all redundancies, *B* takes 15 words to say all that *A* says in 61.

6.2 **PARAGRAPHS**

Having worked out a plan (as explained in Section 4.1) you put it into effect by paragraphing. Each paragraph deals with one section of your subject matter. Paragraph follows paragraph in the order of presentation decided upon in your plan. Clear paragraphing presents the contents of your message in progressive and readily comprehensible stages.

1. *Keep them short*

It is always easier to take in one thing at a time than to try to comprehend several things at once. That is why you must restrict each paragraph to one item or topic. It is also why long paragraphs are a mistake. Try to keep within the limit of five or six short sentences to each paragraph. That is not an absolute rule, but it *is* a useful piece of advice to bear in mind when you are writing.

For their own special purposes, newspapers favour very short paragraphs – *too short* to be suitable for your purposes in much of the practical writing you have to do. But their quick-moving paragraphs are a better model than the cumbersome structure of 'officialese'.

Always begin with a short paragraph. It gets your reader's attention at once. Use it as a 'signpost' of the route that the rest of your message is going to follow.

2. *Give them unity*

Not only must you restrict each paragraph to *one* main point or topic, you must also ensure that each sentence in the paragraph bears on that one point. Don't let any incidental or extraneous matter creep in.

A 'topic sentence' at the beginning of each paragraph helps you to maintain paragraph unity. Like the short first paragraph, it acts as a 'signpost', pointing both writer and reader in the right direction.

3. *Link them*

Although each separate paragraph deals with a distinct item or topic, they all bear on the matter in hand. Each paragraph is there because it makes an important contribution to the subject as a whole. Paragraph links help your reader to see quickly how each paragraph is related to the others and what each contributes to the whole.

When your paragraphs follow each other in chronological, functional or spatial order (see Section 4.1) it is not necessary to provide explicit verbal links. The connections are made apparent by the order of presentation you are following.

When you have chosen to arrange your subject matter in either ascending or descending order of importance (see Section 4.1), verbal links (for example: however; consequently; even so; that is to say; on the contrary) are necessary. Without them, your reader won't know where you are going – and you will probably lose your way.

Exercise 1 *(Answers on page 78)*

This paragraph has a clear topic sentence; and all the other sentences, with one exception, bear on the subject announced there. Identify: (i) the topic sentence; (ii) the sentence that breaks the unity of the paragraph by introducing material which is not relevant to the rest of the paragraph.

The immense technical achievements of nineteenth-century Britain would have been impossible without the work of Henry Bessemer. Up to 1856, steel was an expensive product, imported from Sweden and costing about £50 a ton. Bessemer's system of making steel was still in use well into the twentieth century, though partly replaced by the open hearth process invented by Sir William Siemens. The high price of steel meant that it could be used for only a limited range of manufacture. Bessemer's method, by which cheap pig iron was converted into steel in huge retorts in about half an hour, brought the cost down to £3 a ton. In consequence, steel – stronger and more resilient than iron – was available for the engines, bridges, ships, machinery and railway tracks on which industrial Britain depended.

Exercise 2 *(Suggested answer on page 78)*

Because it is not paragraphed, this report is neither quick to read nor easy to take in. Suggest where paragraph breaks ought to have been made. If you think that certain items ought to have been numbered and 'displayed', make the necessary changes.

Mechanical Carder (c.1789)

As a static display, this machine would not be very interesting. I do not recommend the museum trustees to acquire it for that purpose. For its age, however, it is in good condition. My preliminary inspection suggests that it could be restored to working order without great expense. I can make the following provisional estimates with some confidence. Strip down drive mechanism: £50. Replace worn gearing: £200, if we can find spares; £500, if we have to make a new set. Fit new belt and pulleys: £50. Clean all working parts and reassemble: £30. I have reason to believe that the present owner would accept £60 as a fair price. So, for an outlay of between £390 and £690 (see the second item above) the trustees may be able to acquire a working example of a remarkable invention. If the trustees decide to take this project further, I shall return to the site to make a detailed inspection and then provide firm figures for the necessary restoration work.

CHAPTER 7

NOTES AND SUGGESTED ANSWERS

Chapter 2

Exercise 2

(a) If the writer had tried to put himself in his reader's place, he would not have allowed these *Notes* to be printed in the *Newsletter* in their present state. They are in a fearful muddle.

Their purpose was to inform club members of decisions taken at a meeting - not an easy writing job; and one that cannot be done well unless the subject matter is clearly organised. The writer should have realised that any club member reading an item headed 'Subscriptions' would expect to be told two things: (i) when the annual subscription is due; (ii) whether the subscription rate has been altered.

Having thought that out, he should have arranged his subject matter so that the two items of chief importance were dealt with first:

Item 1: In future, the annual subscription will be due on 1 May. (First paragraph of *Notes*.)

Item 2: The rate of subscription has not been altered. (Second paragraph of *Notes*.)

All other information about the AGM decisions is of secondary importance and should have been presented after those two items.

Instead, the secretary confused his readers by burying the two chief items in a disorganised heap of minor matters, and then he made things even harder for them by omitting to paragraph his *Notes*. A series of short paragraphs (each one devoted solely to one item of information - as in the plan for items 1 and 2, above) would have been a great help.

The secretary will have only himself to blame if his office phone gets red-hot with calls from baffled readers of his badly written *Notes*.

(b) A lively piece of writing - but scatter-brained! The writer feels (and probably *is*) justified in relying on a warm personal relationship with her reader, but she intended her letter to be more than just a friendly, newsy greeting. Practical matters that she was trying to arrange include: a meeting at Euston at a particular time on a particular date; a meeting at a friend's; lunch; theatre tickets; a visit to the theatre; departure on the 20.00 train.

Her reader's reactions to this letter would, in all probability, be something like this:

'A letter from Jean! Nice! I'd like to see her again.'

'Oh, she's coming to London and wants me to meet her. Good!'

'But which day next week does she mean?'

'And what time does the 06.30 from Carlisle arrive at Euston? I suppose I can find out, but she might have saved me the trouble. She must know what time it gets in.'

'And what's this about lunch? Does she plan to have lunch at Jan's, or is she intending to take us out to lunch as well as to the theatre?'

'And which theatre? How can I get tickets when I don't know which theatre she means?'

'She says she's going to be away until the day before the planned outing. That'll be too late to do all the things she's asking me do.'

'Oh, what a mess! I'll have to ring her number every evening next week until I get a reply. Then, I suppose, we can sort something out on the phone.'

'Just like Jean! Always in a muddle!'

Chapter 2

Exercise 3

The instructions require the writer (the candidate) to *give an account of* one of Britain's attempts to renegotiate the terms of its EEC membership. They do *not* tell the candidate to express his/her own opinions. A factual answer is required. The writer is expected to provide the reader (the examiner) with an objective description of whichever particular attempt he/she has chosen to write about.

It follows that the writer should try to show the reader that he/she knows the facts and can set them out clearly.

This answer indicates that the candidate knows the facts, but it fails to set them out clearly. In that respect, it is so badly written that the examiner is bound to make an unfavourable judgement of this candidate's abilities.

First, instead of confining the subject matter to the facts, as the instructions require, the writer digresses into the expression of personal opinions – for example: 'but I take that with a pinch of salt, myself'.

Second, the answer is badly organised. The facts are not set out in a clear order – for example: four 'areas of renegotiation' are mentioned as the main issues under discussion in 1974, but they are described in such a muddled way that the reader has great difficulty in distinguishing each issue from the others. Having referred to two of these main issues, the writer breaks off ('though neither of these ... argued about') before describing the other two in a long-winded and confused addition to the sentence ('and trade with ... were also included').

Then comes another outburst of personal opinion (beginning: 'I'm not at all sure') which obscures the factual and relevant point that the candidate is trying to make (the lost chance to reform CAP). And all this without any paragraphing!

Third, the answer is written in a wholly inappropriate style. The candidate failed to take the writer/reader relationship into account. That relationship (candidate/examiner) is impersonal, and it requires a formal style of writing. The reader will read this answer in his/her official capacity. That capacity (an examiner) is the sole reason for the candidate to write this particular 'message' to this particular person.

That situation does not justify dull, lifeless writing, but it does demand a cool, restrained, formal style. Familiar, colloquial writing ('pinch of salt'; 'I'm not at all sure that it wouldn't'; 'In fact, as it turned out' – and so on) is completely out of place here.

Nor is a personal manner of writing suited to the objective presentation of facts in an ordered sequence. And that was the candidate's main task.

To sum up: the candidate has factual knowledge and is a fluent writer; but his/her misjudgement of the nature of the task and of the writer/reader relationship resulted in a badly written answer.

Chapter 2
Exercise 4

(a) A lively and clear piece of writing – but written for the wrong reader! Sent to a friend, this would be a good letter; but it makes undue demands on its intended reader's tolerance. Chatty throughout, it sounds flippant at times. This is not a suitable tone to use when informing a lecturer of an important academic decision, even though the writer and the reader may be on good terms.

(b) Good, clear writing; but flawed by one blunder when the writer misjudges his readership. Even if the 'joke' about the sun were better than it is (and even if the reader needed to be told that it is meant to be a joke), the writer/reader relationship and the occasion and purpose of writing do not justify would be witty digressions.

Perhaps the writer was uneasy about this misguided attempt to be funny, judging by the way in which the 'seriousness' of the 'joke' is hastily emphasised. In effect, the writer is saying: 'Yes, I know this isn't what you want, so I'll get back to the appropriate way of writing at once. If you read on, you'll see that I know my subject and that I'm dealing with it in a responsible way.'

(c) This over-personalised reply destroys the case that the writer wanted to make. His reader had asked for a reasoned statement of a point of view, but the writer makes no attempt to provide it. This blustering, anecdotal huffing and puffing might be acceptable in late-night *conversation* with like-minded cronies. In the writer/reader relationship of *this* situation, it is most unlikely to persuade the reader to pay serious attention to the writer's opinions.

(d) Oh dear! We must hope that the writer/reader relationship is closer and more affectionate than this piece of writing suggests. The wording ('kind gift' and 'informing you', for example) is cold and distant. And was it necessary to draw a grandparent's attention to the promptness of the letter in quite such a 'business-like' way?

Chapter 3

Exercise 2

This is the letter that Jack Jones wrote to the treasurer. You have studied the way he set about writing it; now see what you think of its contents and style.

> 6 Grange Road
> Byethrop
> BY2 6GR

28 January 19—

Mr H Cash
Hon. Treasurer, Bythrop Social Club
2 Market Square
Bythrop
BY1 2MS

Dear Mr Cash,

Your end-of-year financial statement confirms the strength of the club's position, with a credit balance of over £850 in its current account.

As far as I am aware, we have no immediate commitments to heavy expenditure, so may I suggest that you consider the idea of transferring all funds in excess of £100 into a high-interest deposit account?

The bank is paying 10 per cent gross interest on deposited money, and the club's status as a registered charity would reduce the rate of tax deducted at source. I think I am right in calculating that a real return of rather more than 8 per cent would be available.

As you know, the bank requires three months' notice for the with-drawal of deposited funds, but I do not think that would cause you any problems. It is clear, even to a comparative newcomer, that careful forward planning underpins the management of the club's finances.

Yours sincerely,

Jack Jones

Jack Jones

Chapter 3
Exercise 3

This is the note (memorandum) that Jane Brown wrote. It is a clear and, therefore, an efficient message, suited to the circumstances. Notice that she does not waste time complaining (no whingeing!). Notice, too, that although she is firm, she is polite.

To Fashionparlour   Stitchwood   N. Yorkshire   ST11 2FP
From Jane Brown   11 Garden Close   Mowtown   MW3 11GC
Date   30/4/87
Reference   JB4a12J310S

1 Jumper (wrong colour) and skirt (wrong size) returned herewith.
2 Please replace with goods as specified in my order dated 2/4/87: jumper - colour 1(a) - size 12; skirt - colour 3 - size 10.
3 If the garments ordered are not in stock, please refund my money (P.O. 367421CZ: £19.95).
4 In either case, please refund the return postal charges.

Signed Jane Brown

Chapter 4
Exercise 1

This is the detailed plan that Miss Green finally worked out and on which she based the writing of the information sheet.

1 *Jeavon's Place*
     site - date - who Jeavon was - historical and architectural import-ance of house
2 *Entrance hall*
     oak door and hinges - plasterwork of ceiling - stone fireplace and its fittings

3 *Ground floor rooms*
   dining room (table and sideboard) – parlour (chairs, window seat and chest) – kitchen (utensils, cooking hearth, spit and jack)
4 *Staircase*
   breadth – oak panelling – carved balustrade
5 *1st floor rooms*
   main bedroom (fourposter and its curtains, the great press) – main guest room (best bed for visitors) – smaller rooms (especially 'cot room')
6 *2nd floor rooms*
   small garrets under roof – lack of light – cramped servants' quarters

Note Having worked out a clear plan, Miss Green's remaining problem was how to do justice to her material in not more than 450 words. She managed it by writing economically, compressing the information into as few words as possible. (see Section 4.2 and Chapter 5). Again, she 'telescoped' items whenever she could. For example, she condensed the material in part 6 of her plan into just two short sentences.

Chapter 4
Exercise 2
Having read John Smith's handout, the chairperson put it in the waste-paper basket. Then he did the job himself, like this:

APPLICATION FOR MEMBERSHIP OF THE MUSIC SOCIETY

Procedure

1 Get an application form from the college office.
2 Fill it in and return it as soon as possible.
3 Put it in the society's mailbox (4th floor, Standford Building) not later than noon on Friday 10 October.
4 You will be told by Wednesday 15 October whether you have been successful.

Compare that with the handout you wrote. Which is the better piece of writing?

Chapter 4
Exercise 3
Janet White worked out this plan for her report on the telephones. She grouped the features of each instrument according to their functions, so that the office manager could easily compare them and make a good choice.

1 *Instrument A*
     Features
     (i)   number-calling system
     (ii) memory capacity
     (iii) memory storage and retrieval system
     (iv) repeat-call system
     (v)   bell or call tone
     (vi) mute

She then repeated that structure for instruments *B*, *C* and *D*.

Chapter 4
Exercise 4

(i)   In passage (a) the writer's objective is to obtain the committee's agreement to the proposed action. In passage (b) the writer's objective is to motivate members to join in the recruiting drive.
(ii) The first sentence of (a). The last sentence of (b).
(iii) Descending order of importance in (a). Ascending order of importance in (b).
(iv) In both pieces of writing, the order of presentation is well suited to the nature of the contents and to the writer's objective.

      Passage (a) begins with a crisp statement of the action proposed by the writer. The rest of the passage provides reasoned arguments in support of the recommendation set out in the first sentence. (Note, for example, the expression 'unhappy experiment', which reinforces the previous reasoning.)

      Passage (b) deploys the writer's case persuasively, step by step. Note especially how the writer supplies evidence to prove that the committee has been doing its utmost to recruit new members. By the time members read the last sentence, which asks *them* to take action, they have been persuaded of the importance of recruiting and of their obligation to play their part.

Chapter 5
Exercise 4
(i) corrections; (ii) undertaking; (iii) prudent; (iv) implement; (v) manufacture.

Chapter 5
Exercise 6
Statements (iii), (iv), (v) and (vi) are true.

Chapter 5
Exercise 7
(i) Some users of Rosedrop have told us that it does cover up nasty smells.
(ii) We consider that our opponents' proposals are unrealistic and deceitful.
(iii) Wixwax is a good furniture polish.
(iv) This is our latest offer, which we are sending to everybody on our mailing list. If you apply by 1 April, we will give you a 1 per cent bonus out of the commission we get from Richkwik and Partners for acting as their agents. Because we cannot know whether this investment will be profitable for you or not, we are quoting Richkwik's average results over the past two years, hoping that you will assume that this new offer will do at least as well. You will then rush to buy it.
(v) I do not agree that 'chairperson' is a more objective word than 'chairman'. People who say that it is make me very angry. I have no arguments to use against them, so I will abuse them and sneer at them to encourage you to do so too.

Chapter 5
Exercise 8
(i) We send accounts monthly and require payment within 14 days.
(ii) The planning sub-committee ignored several regulations when granting this application.

Chapter 5
Exercise 9
(i) We had considerable difficulty in getting the panel to register our brand name. (I suppose 'considerable' *does* add to the meaning?)
(ii) We expected the union representatives to be hostile to our latest proposals.

Chapter 5
Exercise 10
(i) We have asked our subcontractors why they have not sent our door locks.
(ii) The threat of unemployment is worrying our workers.

Chapter 5
Exercise 12
(i) Prolonged frost has made the ground too hard for racing, so the stewards have cancelled today's meeting.
(ii) Improved conditions will enable several firms in this region to regain lost export markets.

Chapter 6
Exercise 1
(i) The first sentence.
(ii) The third sentence.

Chapter 6
Exercise 2

Mechanical Carder (c.1789)

As a static display, this machine would not be very interesting. I do not recommend the museum trustees to acquire it for that purpose.

For its age, however, it is in good condition. My preliminary inspection suggests that it could be restored to working order without great expense.

I can make the following provisional estimates with some confidence.

(1) Strip down drive mechanism: £50.
(2) Replace worn gearing: £200, if we can find spares; £500, if we have to make a new set.
(3) Fit new belt and pulleys: £50.
(4) Clean all working parts and reassemble: £30.

I have reason to believe that the present owner would accept £60 as a fair price. So, for an outlay of between £390 and £690 (see item 2), the trustees may be able to acquire a working example of a remarkable invention.

If the trustees decide to take this project further, I shall return to the site to make a detailed inspection and then provide firm figures for the necessary restoration work.